THE BOUNDARIES WORKBOOK

Exercises to Help You Set Healthy Boundaries and Improve Your Relationships

JAKE MORRILL, LMFT

ROCKRIDGE
PRESS

For general information on our other products and services or to obtain technical support, please contact our Customer Care Department within the United States at (866) 744-2665, or outside the United States at (510) 253-0500.

Rockridge Press publishes its books in a variety of electronic and print formats. Some content that appears in print may not be available in electronic books, and vice versa.

Interior and Cover Designer: Linda Kocur
Art Producer: Melissa Malinowsky
Editor: Adrian Potts
Production Editor: Jenna Dutton
Production Manager: Lanore Coloprisco

Paperback ISBN: 978-1-63807-652-0
eBook ISBN: 978-1-63807-666-7
R0

To Ken Shuman, whose coaching on boundaries
helped me live the way I wanted to live.

CONTENTS

INTRODUCTION

Let's get something clear from the start: Boundary-setting isn't about learning how to say "no." Boundary-setting is learning how to say your life's deepest and most powerful "yes." It's about making a commitment, at long last, to the life you want, to the values you cherish and the goals that inspire you. That's what boundaries are for.

Without boundaries, we can trade our whole lives away. For instance, a coaching client I'll call Sarita had always dreamed of visiting the Galapagos Islands. The departure date approached. But then her mother got sick, her kids started fighting, and her ex said that after all, he couldn't take the kids while she was gone. Then her boss threw an unexpected project at her. A week before the trip, stressed and exhausted, pulled in every direction, she canceled her tickets. Maybe some later time she'd go. But not now.

Civil rights leader and spiritual teacher Howard Thurman once wrote: "Don't ask what the world needs. Ask what makes you come alive and go do it. Because what the world needs is people who have come alive."

As a therapist and leadership coach, I work with people like Sarita who look successful on the outside but haven't taken seriously what makes them come alive. To do so, they sometimes think, would be selfish. Or they're scared of disappointing others. So they live with frustration, resentment, and quiet heartbreak.

Here's the good news: People can change. If you've been struggling like Sarita, you can change.

This workbook can change your life. It's a guide to the importance of boundaries, with information about the factors that influence them. You'll learn about setting boundaries in many realms of your life, and you'll learn skills to maintain and adapt those boundaries as needed.

A year after canceling her trip, having worked with me on boundaries, Sarita finally went to the Galapagos Islands and started living the way she'd been meaning to live. I don't know what dream you've been putting on hold, but I do know that better boundaries are the key to the life you've always wanted.

HOW TO USE THIS BOOK

Think of reading this book as like attending a workshop. You're not intended to simply be the audience, receiving these words from a distance. Dive in. Be a participant. Engage with the questions. Apply the ideas to your life. Do the exercises. A person can read a cookbook all afternoon and still be hungry. The same is true here: To develop the boundaries that will give shape to the life that you're seeking, you'll need to get cooking.

Here's what to expect:

◆ Part 1 is an introduction to various types of boundaries and why each is important to a thriving life.
◆ Part 2 offers a range of practical exercises to guide you through the process of setting and maintaining boundaries.

If it helps, you can think of part 1 as "Developing Understanding" and part 2 as "Putting It into Practice." Along the way, you'll encounter Boundaries in Practice sidebars. These provide practical examples of strategies to try right away; they're related to the topic we're discussing at that moment. At the end of each section, you'll find Key Takeaways, so you can review and lock in the major concepts of what you've just read.

Some books are designed as a pick-and-choose buffet. Not this one. This book invites you to read from start to finish, because each section builds on the previous sections. Of course, as you integrate what you read, you can go back to reread earlier sections. The whole book may be reused, too, in different seasons of your life. If the boundary work you're doing this year is helping you establish a foundation, it may be that next year you're further along in the construction process.

Let me be clear about one more thing: This book is not a replacement for mental health treatment. Are you experiencing feelings of anxiety or depression, or are you involved in a destructive or abusive relationship? If so, please seek professional help. There's no shame in getting the help you need. In Resources (page 145), you will find more information about where you can seek assistance.

In closing, I just want to tell you how excited I am for you. I can only imagine what you have been through and what it took to decide to risk making a change. It won't be easy and it will take some practice, but I am certain you can have the life you want, supported and sustained by clear, thoughtful boundaries.

PART ONE

Understanding Boundaries

In the early 1960s, an industrial engineering professor from Yale University reportedly said: "If I had only one hour to solve a problem, I would spend up to two-thirds of that hour in attempting to define what the problem is." He was talking about the industrial manufacturing process, but the same idea can apply to trying to change our lives.

Our enthusiasm for life can lead us to leap before we look, to impulsively act before we understand. But if we want to attain the clarity, purpose, and dignity of a well-defined life, we need to first understand the nature and purpose of boundaries: what they are and why they're important. When we better understand the mountain we're preparing to climb, our inevitable setbacks and stumbles won't be confusing or frustrating. They'll be chances to learn, to integrate what we've learned, and to move forward again even stronger than before.

CHAPTER 1

What Are Boundaries?

My father-in-law is a retired environmental science teacher. When he walks through the woods, he knows the name of every tree and how it relates to the wider ecosystem. As for me, I can hardly tell the difference between an oak and an aspen. So when we walk through the same forest, he and I have different experiences. When we know the world by name, we can relate to it more mindfully. The same goes for boundaries.

Think of this chapter as a field guide identifying different types of boundaries and their component parts. As you become familiar with them, you'll navigate the forest of life with more clarity and purpose.

Defining Boundaries

Just as a nation passes laws to define what is, and what is not, acceptable within its borders, you have the right and responsibility to sovereignty, or self-governance; to define what is and isn't acceptable within you. Boundaries are the intentional choices you make to define yourself. Boundaries say "This is mine" and "That is not mine." Boundaries define responsibilities, too, saying, "This is what I will be responsible for" and "This is what I will not be responsible for."

Whereas a boundaryless life can leave you exhausted—continually bargaining with others and yourself—a life with well-defined boundaries is energizing. The clarity of direction and limits in such a life allow you to channel your energy and emotion into pursuing the life you desire. Clarity within yourself, over time, teaches others how to relate to you more clearly, as well. For example, if a boundary for you is that you don't go to scary movies, people will stop asking you to go see scary movies. On the other hand, if you're clear that you want to see only scary movies, people will seek you out to go see them. Defining yourself clearly is not only a gift to you, it's also a gift to others (even if, in the short term, they're disappointed that you won't go along with whatever they want to do).

Of course, boundaries aren't only about your preferred movie genre. Your own body, and especially your own sexuality, is a profound area of boundary-setting. Having clarity about what will and won't happen with your body is liberating. As we explore further, we'll see that defining yourself clearly through mindful boundaries presents opportunities in every sphere of life, from work to family to social life to how you relate to yourself.

Myths and Misconceptions

In a society oriented toward feeling good, there can be a myth that boundaries are unkind. After all, clear boundaries are meant not to promote warm, communal feelings but to ensure individual clarity, safety, and freedom.

The truth is that boundaries can raise anxiety, in you and in others. When anxiety goes up, the ability to think clearly goes down. When it comes to relationships, anxious people have a hard time imagining two well-defined people, responsible for their own boundaries, thoughtfully coordinating how they will relate. Instead, anxiety tells them that people must move in lockstep, agreeing on everything. Anxiety says, "I can't be happy unless you're happy. I can't act unless you act the same way."

Most common myths about boundaries flow from an anxiety-driven view of relationships. For instance, say someone wants to go to a movie and the other person doesn't. Because an anxiety-driven view of relationships says both people need to want the same thing at the same time, anxiety would see someone saying "no" to the movie as hurtful.

A similar myth is that boundaries are selfish. In fact, boundaries are generous and caring. Think of it this way: If I never tell you what I really want but only ever go along with what I think makes you happy, will you ever truly know me? Or will you only know the disguise I wear as I am trying to meet your needs? Boundaries allow others to know who you really are.

There's a myth that to be legitimate, boundaries need to be the same all the time. Well, that's silly. My boundaries with my kids are not the same as my boundaries with telemarketers. Different relationships have different boundaries. My boundaries with my kids regarding cleaning their rooms are different from my boundaries with them regarding homework help. The same relationship can have different boundaries in different contexts. And generally, my boundaries for helping them now, as teens, are different from what they were years ago when my kids were little. The same relationships can have different boundaries at different times.

BOUNDARIES IN PRACTICE

Consider an upcoming event you feel obliged to attend: a family gathering, a work meeting, or something else. Let's practice reframing—adopting a different perspective—to change "have to" to "want to." How could you reframe the dreaded event so that it serves your purposes? If you were attending to serve yourself, what would be your goal? (What could you learn? What would you want to try?) To support that goal, what limits or boundaries would you set? For instance, at a family barbecue, where you can predict there will be pressure to eat certain foods or a certain amount, can you eat what and how you decide to? As you pursue this goal and uphold these boundaries, who would be upset, and how would you respond? For now, this is only a thought exercise, to begin imagining a life where you're in the driver's seat.

Personal Boundaries

Someone can have boundaries about what they will and won't do in any sphere of their life: with sleep, with diet, with anything. But personal boundaries—the limits and rules we set within relationships—are perhaps the most challenging to identify and uphold. They're challenging because we define them in relation to other people who are, likewise, defining their own boundaries (or avoiding the work of defining their own boundaries), and our desire to please or soothe others can confuse our own efforts to get clear for ourselves.

There are three main types of personal boundaries: rigid, porous, and healthy. It may seem that healthy is the only way to go, but, in fact, there are times when a rigid or porous boundary can be helpful. This section will define these three types of boundaries and how they may be applied.

Rigid

One of the world's tallest buildings, the Willis Tower, stands in Chicago, which is known as the Windy City because of the gusts that come off Lake Michigan with tremendous force. Under such conditions, if the Willis Tower was built to be rigid, it would break. But architect Fazlur Rahman Khan designed in the capacity for the tower to sway up to three feet in any direction.

Boundaries, too, are stronger when they respond to the environment. But rigid boundaries are iron-clad rules that a person upholds regardless of the situation. Like most rigid things, rigid boundaries are brittle, seemingly always at risk.

Because a person with rigid boundaries is oriented toward their own rules, rather than their environment, they often maintain a personal distance from others. Even if they want to meet an old friend, they'll decline the opportunity if their own rule says "no." They attempt to live in emotional isolation. They won't ask for help. Rigid boundaries are a cage they build for themselves.

Why would someone build such a cage? People often adopt rigid boundaries because they don't trust themselves to hold those boundaries under pressure. This is likely when they have experienced violation of their boundaries earlier in life. So, rigid boundaries can be a way to practice being in control of themselves, for a while. In that way, they can be a useful stopgap, like using training wheels when learning to ride a bike. But in the long run, rigid boundaries don't give us control; they end up controlling us.

Porous

At the beach, my kids like to build enormous sandcastles with heavy walls that seem as if they could stop anything. But when the tide rises, the walls wash away. Porous boundaries are like that. A person can figure out exactly what their boundaries will be, only for those boundaries to then dissolve like a sandcastle in the tide when they encounter anyone else.

If rigid boundaries distance a person from others, porous boundaries do the opposite. A person with porous boundaries always puts other people's needs first. Say you've got a deadline on a project, but your neighbor asks you to babysit their kid. If you've got porous boundaries, you'll say "yes" without thinking.

If clear boundaries distinguish between my responsibility and yours, porous boundaries confuse that distinction. Someone with porous boundaries will automatically take on someone else's burdens and challenges. Porous boundaries create a need for everyone else to be okay—or sometimes, for particular people to be okay. Such an unguarded, anxious stance can contribute to accepting disrespect, poor treatment, and even abuse, because the person with porous boundaries has a hard time setting limits or saying "no."

Someone with porous boundaries is also often unable to hear the limits set by someone else. Such a person will overshare, seeking to shift some responsibility for their own problems onto whoever will accept it.

There are times when experimenting with porous boundaries can be helpful. If you've primarily relied on rigid boundaries and leaned heavily on the word "no," it can be a useful experiment to try living with a more open "yes" for a time. The purpose is to notice what possibilities present themselves when "no" isn't your default answer, and also to practice mindfully tending your boundaries when you've said "yes" to someone else's proposal. Even though you give an initial "yes," you have the right to say "no" or renegotiate at any point after that. Some practice with more porous boundaries can provide practice for that midstream renegotiation.

That said, in general, porous boundaries come from the unwillingness or inability of a person to establish clear, thoughtful boundaries. Because a person with porous boundaries is controlled by the need to please and avoid disconnection, they will sacrifice much, including their values and goals.

Healthy

Whereas rigid and porous boundaries are fantasy-based, healthy boundaries are reality-based. Someone with rigid boundaries imagines that isolating from others will protect them; someone with porous boundaries imagines that people-pleasing will protect them. But a person with healthy boundaries knows that well-being is not found from defending themselves in these ways against imagined threats. Rather, well-being is found by engaging the realities and tensions of a complicated world. In that light, there are two paired qualities of healthy boundaries: being responsible for yourself and being responsive to others.

To be responsible for yourself requires clarity about your own personal needs and wants, and the capacity to convey those needs and wants to others. If you need a nap and a shower after work before going out to dinner, but you never say so, it's not fair to be cranky if your partner suggests leaving earlier. You're responsible for knowing your needs and communicating them.

In the same situation, if your partner responds that they are concerned about arriving at the restaurant later in the evening, when there might be a longer wait, you're not obliged to surrender your needs. In fact, not compromising on what's important to you is a standard of healthy boundaries. But you are responsible for responding to your partner's feedback and perhaps engaging in creative problem-solving to incorporate both your need for a nap and a shower and your partner's need not to have a long wait at the restaurant. That's what being responsible and responsive looks like: honoring yourself and also responding mindfully to others.

BOUNDARY ASSESSMENT

As you consider your own relationship to boundaries thus far in your life, it will help to take stock and assess how rigid, porous, or healthy your boundaries are. Use these questions to reflect on what kinds of personal boundaries you keep.

So you can protect what's important to you, what do you do to keep alert to your own wants and needs?

What are five important wants and needs in your life? How do you honor and uphold those? How do you neglect them?

Because others in your life are not mind readers, how do you communicate those important needs and wants to them?

For a person with porous boundaries, it's painful to tolerate differences in feelings and wants. When something's important to you, how do you tolerate differences with, the disappointment of, and disapproval from other people?

A person with rigid boundaries insists on following their own rules, no matter what else is going on. When is a time you have maintained your own values but also adapted how you applied them in response to a change in the situation or in response to another person?

Types of Boundaries

We've discussed the nature and purpose of boundaries and different characteristics of boundaries—rigid, porous, and healthy. Now let's apply what we've learned to different dimensions of human experience: physical, emotional, sexual, intellectual, material, and time.

As we do, think about your own boundary-keeping. Different people will struggle and shine in different contexts. For instance, someone with healthy physical boundaries may have porous boundaries regarding time.

Our particular relationship to boundaries isn't mere happenstance. Each of us has been shaped by our experience in the environments we've known. Each of us has learned which behaviors contribute to our own survival. Sometimes, our experience in an environment with confusing or even harmful boundaries has shaped our behavior so that now, years later, our own boundaries in a certain aspect of life are troubling, or at least obsolete.

That's understandable. In fact, it's human. And although humans are shaped by past experiences, we can also learn and practice so that our lives take on a new shape, one that we have chosen. What you've experienced in your past, which has produced the current boundaries you have (which you developed back then for your own survival), need not determine how you'll live going forward. With that encouragement, let's look at boundaries in these different settings.

Physical

Physical boundaries address how we protect our sovereignty over our own bodies. Sovereignty addresses internal and external considerations.

Internally, physical self-governance is about how we are aware of, and tend to, the needs of our bodies—for instance, the need for rest and sleep, our diets, and our water intake. Decisions about health care and health maintenance, such as exercise, are the responsibility of anyone with a body.

Sovereignty also includes external considerations, such as how to relate with others. This encompasses our boundaries regarding physical touch: how much, what kind, by whom, for how long, in what settings. Physical boundaries arise regarding activities with others, as well. We may choose to swing dance but not to play rugby or go skydiving. What our bodies will do and will not do is up to each one of us.

Emotional

The first day of my therapy graduate program, the professor asked the students to each share three important things about our lives. The first person shared three profound experiences, including a deep violation that she had survived. The second person followed in line, speaking with great feeling.

What I'll never forget was the woman who came next. She said, "I'm here in this program to learn how to become a therapist, not to get or give personal therapy in the classroom. I have my own therapist already. For now, I'm not willing to disclose sensitive personal information to a room full of people I have not met before." There was a thoughtful silence in the room as we all reflected on how we would, or would not, disclose our emotions in this context. She had reminded us that we had a choice.

Emotional boundaries ask you to be mindful about how, when, and with whom you express your emotions or disclose your emotional experiences. As my fellow student demonstrated, it's perfectly acceptable for one person in a group to choose boundaries that are different from what others choose.

You can also choose what emotions you're willing to receive from others at any given time. Because emotions can be so unwieldy, people can sometimes rush to either rigid or porous boundaries, insisting on no emotional disclosure or else insisting on dumping unprocessed emotions on others, regardless of context. But, as elsewhere, when it comes to what emotions you're willing to receive from others, your responsibility for your own healthy emotional boundaries will ask you to adopt a more thoughtful stance than "all or nothing."

Sexual

In some ways, we are sexual beings our whole lives long. Each of us is responsible for our own sexual boundaries. That takes discernment within yourself and discussion with your partner(s).

Sexual relations, from beginning to end, require people to be free to make the choices that serve their desires and express care for one another. And that requires communicating boundaries and agreeing on what boundaries will be upheld as a condition of intimacy.

The primary boundary in healthy sexual relations is active, ongoing consent. Because each of us is sovereign over our own body, each partner is responsible for deciding and communicating what will and won't happen, sexually, with their body. And each partner may amend or reverse that decision at any time. Just because someone says "yes" to something doesn't mean they can't say, "Well, on second thought, no," a few minutes later. Or vice versa.

To give consent, you must be in touch with your own sexual needs and preferences in such a way that it's clear what you will consent to. To gain consent from your partner, you must make clear requests and be able to hear either "yes" or "no" from your partner, with deep respect. Pressure, coercion, and other forms of manipulation make true consent impossible.

Sexual boundaries continue beyond sexual activity itself. For instance, each partner has a right to the level of privacy they choose regarding their sexual activity. A partner's loose talk about it to others would be a violation of those sexual boundaries.

Intellectual

To paraphrase the late senator Daniel Moynihan, "You are entitled to your opinion. But you are not entitled to your own facts." But sometimes it seems as if we're living in a "post-truth" era, when people base their opinions on very different sets of what they believe to be facts. Philosophers might call it an "epistemological crisis"—a crisis of not knowing what's true or how to agree on what's true.

In such a time, it's important to define your intellectual boundaries regarding what sources you consult, what arguments you will pursue, what proof you will require as you determine for yourself what is true or not. Someone with healthy and not rigid intellectual boundaries will also know how and when they will change their mind.

Intellectual boundaries apply to not only how to relate to the truth but also how to exchange ideas. In an exchange, some people insist only on their own claims about the truth, whereas others are desperate for everyone to agree, regardless of what they personally believe. Healthy intellectual boundaries relating to others are built on respect, tolerance, and the willingness to understand, without the need to convert others or the fear of being converted. When a person stands for their beliefs and convictions and yet also remains in dialogue with others who may not share those beliefs and convictions, we see a principled and free mind at work—a person exercising healthy intellectual boundaries. Especially in a "post-truth" era, a person who upholds clear intellectual boundaries may challenge others to do the same.

Material

Just as oversharing or undersharing personal information in a relationship can be a sign of anxiety-driven boundaries, rather than healthy ones, the same is true about money and other material items. We can imagine a relationship in which someone is far too loose with their money and possessions—paying for every meal, buying inappropriately expensive gifts. On the other hand, we can also imagine someone who declines to share anything they own or pay for anything for others.

Being mindful and clear about who is responsible for what, and when items that are owned may be used by others and under what conditions and when, are healthy boundaries. For example, I know someone who owns a pickup truck. He's happy for friends from church to borrow it for community volunteer projects, as long as they tell him a few days in advance, use it for volunteer service, return it before dinnertime on the same day, and fill up the tank before they bring it back.

That list of conditions is an excellent model of healthy boundaries. What are healthy are not the particular boundaries he's set—a person could imagine reasonable variations on any of those boundaries. What's healthy is the thoughtfulness and clarity of the boundaries. The clear expectations mean others can actually borrow the truck without having to wonder whether the owner is secretly seething, regretting his choice.

As you think of valuable items you own, for example a car or a musical instrument, or about money itself, think about your own boundaries. What will you share, with whom, under what conditions, and when?

Time

We may all know someone who is forever rushing from one thing to the next, eager to address one thing, then another, all for somebody else. As with our own body and our intellectual and material life, we are each responsible for governing our own time. When we're busy, it's tempting to lay blame on others for how we use our time. But in calmer moments, we know that we have much more choice about how to govern our time than we may have thought. We may choose to devote a certain amount of time and not more to volunteering. Or to certain relationships. Or to work. In each of these realms, as others push us to overfunction, it takes work to stay committed to how we've sworn to spend our time.

Boundaries around time will require priorities about how you'll spend your day, which tasks you'll take on, and how much time you'll give to certain realms of life—work versus family, for instance. How much rest and self-care time you need and take is a boundary issue, as well.

Punctuality and timeliness are also boundary questions about time. How will you uphold your agreements about time with others, knowing your time management also affects their ability to uphold clear standards for their time?

At the broadest level, you may decide how much time you're willing to give to a relationship, a project, or a career, and know that your decisions about those commitments are made because life is short.

Key Takeaways

Before going deeper into working on your own boundaries, it's helpful to first learn about them and to clear up misconceptions:

1. Rigid boundaries are rule-bound, brittle, and isolate a person from others.

2. Porous boundaries come from an urge for sameness and togetherness, and the pain of difference.

3. Healthy boundaries come from awareness of your own needs and preferences and are integrated calmly and consistently into your behavior, as well as being communicated to others in a way they can understand.

4. Our particular boundaries, for good or ill, are not happenstance. They come from our childhood efforts to survive in environments that could sometimes be confusing. But our long-standing patterns are not our destiny; we can change.

5. We can define our personal boundaries across many important realms of life. Physical, emotional, sexual, intellectual, material, and time boundaries are some examples.

6. For each of these dimensions, we may have different boundaries for different situations, different relationships, and even different moments within the same relationship. They are *our* boundaries. *We* get to decide.

CHAPTER 2

Why Are Boundaries Important?

Modern society thrills to rule-breakers. For instance, the movie trope of the bad cop reinforces the narrative that those who break the rules usually win in the end. Entertaining as they may be on the screen, these forces of chaos don't provide a blueprint for life. Rebellion can become as much of a habit as compliance. The real maverick, it turns out, is the one who charts their own course, rooted in the integrity of a well-defined life that is given shape by clear boundaries. This chapter explores why it matters so much to be able to live like this.

The Benefits of Setting Boundaries

Setting boundaries is hard. Is it worth it? Well, imagine a boat in the middle of the ocean without an engine, sail, or rudder. It might stay afloat but it would not make much progress, other than where the swells of the ocean happened to direct it. Another boat, equipped with the capacity to power itself through the waves, could go wherever its captain chose. Because a life with clear boundaries is like that second boat, the person at the wheel of their life will experience the benefits of better mental and emotional health, and better relationships that are rooted in freedom and empowerment.

Mental and Emotional Health

Mental and emotional well-being come from the sense that our needs will be met and that we will be safe. Boundaries go a long way toward ensuring both. For instance, when you know how much sleep you need and can protect that boundary, you won't be vulnerable to pressures from others to trade away that precious time, and you will engage with life well rested.

When you are clear on other needs, too—for food, water, time to think, and so forth—and are able to assert those needs, you'll live a different life than someone who regularly trades away their own needs to please other people. Emotionally and physically, your ability to uphold clear boundaries regarding the potentially violating behavior of others will also increase the chances of you feeling and being safe. The refusal to tolerate unwanted touch or unacceptable emotional behavior, such as manipulation or blame, will unhook you from the depleting drama created by others.

Furthermore, when you have clear boundaries, you won't doubt yourself after an encounter in what can be (for some) a familiar cycle of second-guessing. When you keep your boundaries, you're always clear on what's okay and what's not okay, avoiding the tortuous process of trying to figure things out in the moment.

When you're clear on what brings you joy and what brings you pain, and can act accordingly, you are regularly rewarded. A life in which you take your own needs seriously and gravitate toward life-giving interactions while protecting yourself against harmful ones is a life that, over time, accrues more of the benefits of mental and emotional health.

Autonomy and Independence

When you govern yourself with clear boundaries, you experience greater autonomy and independence. Clarity of mind allows clarity of choice. Choices bring consequences, but they're consequences a person with good boundaries has decided are worth it.

Over time, the exercise of autonomy and independence creates identity. For instance, a friend of mine works with organizational leaders. Recently she told me, "People don't come to me for questions about management or operations. They come to me to talk about relationships in the workplace. That's my focus." Do you hear how clear her professional identity is? Her clarity has sometimes meant loss of business from people who'd want her to work on a project outside of her mission. But over the years, as she's consistently said "yes" to the work that is hers to do and "no" to the work that isn't, her identity has shined brighter and brighter in the workplace.

Clear boundaries don't only help you establish and assert a well-defined identity; they also help others relate to you better. Think about it: When someone's identity is clear and vivid, it's a lot easier to relate to them, rather than trying to read their mind or to guess what they're like. A person with solid boundaries doesn't create the kind of confusion that people-pleasing habits can create. Relationships thrive in the context of clear boundaries.

Finally, boundaries create conditions of personal freedom. Instead of forever depending on others to meet your needs, the well-defined life means you make sure your own needs are taken care of.

What Happens in a Life Without Boundaries?

If a well-defined life provides well-being and safety, thriving relationships, and freedom, a boundaryless life leaves one vulnerable to exactly the opposite. When a person isn't able to establish clear boundaries, they're often at the mercy of situations and the whims of others. Such a person feels resentment; they feel disrespected and blame others for how things are. It's a life that feels out of control, which can be frightening and exhausting.

Yes, boundary-keeping can be uncomfortable in the short term. But boundary-lessness means the ongoing pain of a life that's determined by other people and circumstances.

Stress, Anxiety, and Burnout

Because a life without boundaries is a life in which you are vulnerable to the ongoing incursions of others, it is plagued by chronic stress. Evolutionarily, stress has a protective function, but our bodies were never designed to be stressed all the time.

One way to understand stress is through the primal fight-or-flight response—the physiological survival mechanism that prepares the body to respond to a threat. In fight-or-flight mode, blood rushes to the large muscle groups, our vision narrows, our heart rate increases, and our level of the hormone cortisol rises. Cortisol isn't necessarily bad (for instance, it aids in tissue repair). But sustained elevated cortisol levels from chronic stress are linked to problems such as high blood pressure, heart disease, headaches, weight gain, memory impairment, depression, and ongoing anxiety.

Rather than activating the fight-or-flight response appropriately to the occasional presence of actual threats, when you live a life without boundaries, you are forever compelled to be on guard against a world that seems generally threatening. Because it requires a lot of resources to sustain that level of vigilance, the chronic anxiety of the boundaryless life can be, quite literally, exhausting.

Although tireless workers (or parents or neighbors) are usually admired and praised, in fact, they're often overwhelmed and inevitably burn out. For instance, someone who is unable to set limits or say "no" to workplace demands may be able to function at a high level for some time, but gradually that expenditure of energy without counterbalancing rewards or renewal will catch up with them. That's how boundarylessness leads, in time, to burnout.

Misplaced Energy

Imagine you have planned to spend your Saturday reading a book. But then a neighbor asks for help moving a couch, and you agree. Then a friend invites you to a movie that you know you won't like, but you say, "Yes, of course." Your mother keeps you on the phone for an hour, complaining. Then you finish a few tasks your coworker didn't finish on Friday. Soon enough, it's Saturday night and you've spent the whole day fulfilling other people's needs. Now, imagine that most days are like that. Rather than using your time and energy to read a book, or pursue goals that you yourself set, you redirect your energy to serving other people's projects and preferences.

It's not merely the inability to say "no" that leads to this kind of life. It's also a failure to clarify and protect your own goals and priorities that can produce ongoing dissatisfaction and frustration.

The same happens in relationships. A person without boundaries will orient themselves to whatever seems to keep others happy. In the moment, of course, that can be soothing for everyone. But over time, without boundaries, relationships suffer. The person who is unwilling to set boundaries will often adopt passive-aggressive tactics, trying to bait their partner into reading their mind or fulfilling their needs, without ever having communicated directly what those needs are. The other person in such a relationship will become wary, unsure of what they can trust with someone who is unwilling to articulate their own needs, values, or priorities.

Finances can also suffer from boundarylessness. When you aren't able to make long-term decisions that are based on clear principles, your relationship to money will be impulsive, fear-based, and ultimately, unsustainable. Living without boundaries can end up costing a lot of time, tension, and money.

Boundary Violations

A boundary violation occurs when someone else asserts control over what is rightly yours to govern. Such violations can take the form of financial or professional exploitation in the public sphere, but the most common and intimate forms of violation are verbal, emotional (or psychological), and physical. These violations are especially harmful because, rather than damaging your status or role, they damage your dignity and selfhood. A violator, of course, is responsible for their violations. But your own ability to set and keep boundaries can do a lot to help protect you from violations.

Verbal

Proponents of free speech sometimes defend their right to say anything. Certainly, people may say whatever they like, however they like. But behavior comes with consequences, including others refusing to engage anymore. When someone uses inflammatory, deliberately inaccurate, or derogatory language, they violate the norms of reasonable, respectful dialogue. The same is true of gossip. To maintain the social space for everyone, people may rightly disallow such damaging speech in order to promote responsible, productive discourse. You wouldn't allow a toddler throwing a tantrum to take an entire room hostage; the same goes for a person who violates the norms of verbal respect.

Just as boundaries support the functioning of a group's conversational space, they also help uphold the dignity of interpersonal relationships. When someone resorts to bullying tactics, such as a raised voice or shouting, or other kinds of attempts to silence someone else, such as mockery, it's healthy to cease any engagement that would implicitly normalize such behavior and to insist on more responsible ways of interacting. If you don't interrupt these kinds of verbal violations by setting clear boundaries on what kinds of interactions you will and will not participate in, you are vulnerable to continuing to be on the receiving end of it.

BOUNDARIES IN PRACTICE

Consider this scenario: A coworker, Chad, interrupts you regularly in meetings. Another coworker agrees it's annoying, but no one is willing to stop it. Although you might fantasize about a public showdown, as you begin to practice boundary-setting, a first step could be to ask Chad for a private, one-on-one meeting in which you share four things: what you observe, how it makes you feel, how you'd prefer meetings to go, and what you are requesting of him going forward. Then you can hear his perspective. You need not come to a position of agreement. This is only practicing clearly communicating your boundaries.

Psychological and Emotional

The 1944 psychological thriller *Gaslight*, starring Ingrid Bergman and Charles Boyer, tells the story of a husband who gradually convinces his wife that she is going insane. The movie spawned the concept of "gaslighting," which is the attempt to manipulate someone into doubting their own firsthand view of reality. Other forms of manipulation include corrosive criticism, shaming, demeaning, lying, and bullying—behaviors that seek to control and diminish the other. These are all types of psychological and emotional violation.

A well-defined relationship is characterized by cooperative coordination between peers, each doing their part. A relationship that regresses to domination is one that lacks the boundaries that protect a person's selfhood. For instance, a husband might make "jokes" about his wife's intelligence, or a friend might say that "everyone was laughing at what you wore last night." A boss might direct an employee to perform tasks designed to humiliate the employee. These behaviors can be subtle and may be fully understood only in context, but the impact is clear: The person on the receiving end feels embarrassed, confused, and violated. It's possible to create boundaries that protect against such behavior, including ending a relationship with someone who is unwilling to stop violating psychological boundaries. Often, that kind of action requires support from friends, family, a community, or a professional.

Physical

Many people think of physical boundaries as having to do with who touches their body, when, and how. But physical boundaries extend beyond that, to the personal space around your body, and also to how and when someone else may use or touch your belongings. Physical boundaries include questions of privacy, too.

Of all the types of boundary violations, physical ones are the most upsetting because they are the most intimate. Unwanted touch, including unwanted sexualized touch, is perhaps the most intimate boundary violation there is.

Sometimes, establishing and maintaining physical boundaries is a challenge because of the intense pressure from someone else. Sometimes upholding these boundaries is a challenge because we've had hurtful experiences that created confusion about appropriate physical boundaries. But make no mistake: Everyone has the right to control what happens to their own body and their own possessions.

A well-defined view of what will and what won't happen with your body and your possessions is the opposite of turning away from connection with others. In fact, developing clear physical boundaries can allow you to more deeply engage in intimate relationships with others, because you're confident about what you want and what you don't want, and you won't second-guess yourself at every step.

Key Takeaways

In this chapter, you've learned a lot about why boundaries are important. Before you move on to look at how to create healthy boundaries, let's look at the key takeaways from what you've read so far:

1. Boundaries give life clear direction and purpose.

2. Setting boundaries that take your needs and goals seriously will improve your mental health over time. Consider the cost to your mental health of insufficient boundaries.

3. Establishing clear boundaries will heighten autonomy and reduce your dependence on others. What would your life look like with greater freedom?

4. Chronic stress, leading to burnout, is one of the consequences of boundary-less dependence on others to provide safety and well-being.

5. Boundarylessness leads to wasted hours spent on meeting others' agendas.

6. You have the right to set boundaries about how others speak to you. It's possible to put a halt to verbal boundary violations.

7. Psychological boundary violations are not normal or okay. You need not tolerate gaslighting or shaming behavior by others.

8. You have the right to determine what happens to your body and your belongings.

PART TWO

Establishing Your Boundaries

Part 1 made the case for boundaries: what they are, how they give shape to our lives, the benefits they bring, and the costs that can come from a boundaryless life. In other words, part 1 answered the questions "What?" and "Why?" Part 2 is, perhaps, more practical. Think of it as seeking to answer the question "How?"

In this part, you'll read about how a person's influences inform their relationship with boundaries. You'll see what it looks like to set boundaries and communicate them to others. Finally, you'll learn about boundary maintenance: what it takes to stay faithful to the life you've chosen, over time. The well-defined life isn't only declaring the life we wish we could someday maybe have. It's the practice of actually giving shape to that life and aiming to keep the integrity of that intention, knowing just how precious it is.

CHAPTER 3

Shaping Your Boundaries

Each of us is shaped by deep and powerful influences, from our cultural heritage to our trauma histories. Each of us makes our choices and determines our boundaries in the context of our own value system and our goals for our life. Boundary-setting doesn't happen in a vacuum. As we determine the boundaries that will give shape to our lives, we'll find ourselves in creative exploration (and mindful negotiation) with a range of variables that have, thus far, made us who we are. This chapter invites you to consider the formational influences your own boundary-setting process will engage.

Your Influences

Imagine one person who was raised in a household where clear boundaries were celebrated. Now imagine another person from a household where boundaries were seen as a threat and where relationships were marked by confusion. As adults, these two people would have different processes for setting boundaries. That's true of past influences, and it's also true in the present. Some people will find themselves in relationships and settings that support boundary-setting; for others, setting boundaries will be like moving through hurricane-force winds that are determined to knock them down.

Being aware of these influences, both past and present, will help you anticipate and recognize particular challenges you may face as you work toward giving clear shape to the boundaries in your life. Boundaries are never one-size-fits-all; they are always worked out for a particular life, from particular circumstances, to serve particular values. Your boundaries aren't anybody else's—they're yours. Knowing where you came from will help you know how to get where you want to go.

Heritage and Culture

Through a community-wide interfaith effort, I made friends with a Muslim woman who seemed to know everyone from a wide range of faith communities. She would greet each person she met by name and ask after their kids. But one time, when we were greeting each other, I reached out to shake her hand—and was surprised. She drew her hand up to her chest and nodded and smiled instead. She was following a common Muslim practice, which is that unrelated people of different genders avoid physical contact. My admiration for her, already high, increased even more. Here was someone who could move confidently through a culturally diverse setting while also maintaining the self-possession to follow her own principles and boundaries.

Every person alive is shaped by their culture. People who've been exposed to different cultures will realize that it's often easier to notice norms in cultures that aren't your own. That's why people from minority cultures—those whose norms do not prevail in a particular setting—are often more conscious of the role culture plays than are people of dominant cultures, who tend to see their behaviors as normal and not the product of their culture. People in dominant cultures often think of their behavior as "just how things are."

Culture is a strong influence—but it isn't fate. Even people steeped in traditional cultures make choices about how they will or won't relate to certain norms. An identity forged in cultural practice can be powerful, but only if it's chosen intentionally. Someone who automatically and unthinkingly follows cultural practice has not yet done the work of figuring out how they themself will live. The same could be said of someone who automatically rejects the entirety of their culture outright.

FAMILY AND CULTURAL INFLUENCES

This exercise invites you to reflect on your family and culture of origin. For each category, identify a norm you learned, how it helps you, and how it holds you back. For instance, perhaps in your family there was an expectation to always help others before helping yourself. You may note that this helps you now to be a kind and considerate person to whom people turn in times of need. You might also note that this limits you at times because you tend to neglect your own needs when caring for others.

Perhaps you grew up in more than one culture or family. If that's true for you, you can note differences here or re-create the table for each culture or family in a separate notebook, observing how you've made choices between the respective influences or have chosen to integrate aspects of them.

	NORM(S) OF MY FAMILY OR CULTURE	HOW THIS HELPS ME NOW	HOW THIS LIMITS ME
Dress and appearance			

Continued ➤

Continued ➤

	NORM(S) OF MY FAMILY OR CULTURE	HOW THIS HELPS ME NOW	HOW THIS LIMITS ME
Showing respect			
Family roles			
Helping others			
Work habits and practices			

	NORM(S) OF MY FAMILY OR CULTURE	HOW THIS HELPS ME NOW	HOW THIS LIMITS ME
Expressing opinions and feelings			
Gender roles			
Money and finances			
Saying "no" to others			

A CLOSER LOOK AT CULTURAL PRACTICES

As the story goes, a husband and wife were preparing dinner. The husband cut off a corner of the ham and threw it away before putting it in the oven. "Why do you always do that?" asked the wife. Her husband said, "I don't know. My mother always did it." When he next saw his mother, he asked, "Mom, why do you always cut off a corner of the ham before putting it in the oven?" To which she replied, "I don't know. My mother always did it." The two then went to the man's grandmother and asked her about it. The grandmother said, "If I didn't cut off a corner, the ham never would've fit in the pan I had."

Often, we continue inherited behaviors without knowing their original purpose. In this exercise, do some research. Pick a particular cultural practice that's familiar to you. Now, spend a little bit of time researching how that practice got started: where and when, in what context, and for what purpose. Briefly summarize what you find here.

_____

_____

_____

_____

As you clarify the practice's original purpose, ask yourself: Does this practice have the same purpose for me? Based on what I have learned, how will I relate to the practice going forward? Will I continue it not only because others before me did it, but also because I've made a conscious choice? Explore your thoughts here.

_____

_____

_____

_____

Trauma

When Shauna was eight years old, she was sexually abused by a family member. This person was beloved by others in the family, so Shauna kept quiet, until finally she told her therapist when she was 25—two years after her abuser had died. By then, Shauna had developed some deep patterns of behavior associated with trauma.

Trauma isn't an event; it's a response to an event, whether a violation such as abuse, an accident, or a natural disaster such as an earthquake. There are three kinds of trauma:

1. Acute trauma comes from a single event.

2. Chronic trauma comes from repeated events, such as living with domestic violence.

3. Complex trauma comes from varied and ongoing events, such as the experience of racism or living in a war zone.

In the immediate aftermath of a traumatizing event, people can experience shock or denial. With therapy, many are able to move forward in life. Others, for a variety of reasons—the nature of the event, complicating factors in their background, or recurrence of the event—aren't able to move forward but remain trapped in cognitive and behavioral patterns that are meant to protect them but that can actually be debilitating.

Boundaries are especially important, and often especially challenging, for people with trauma. The events that produced trauma have, in some way, violated the person's sense of selfhood and safety. This is true even when the trauma was not caused by abuse—for example, something like surviving a tornado that destroyed the family home. So developing boundaries, which helps build confidence in their own ability to establish safety, is important. However, because they have experienced profound boundary violations, establishing boundaries can be especially challenging. People with posttraumatic stress disorder (PTSD) can experience hypervigilance, forever scanning the environment for threats, ever on the ready to defend against attack. It is very difficult for them to feel safe.

With support, Shauna developed the capacity to identify and uphold her own important boundaries, even in a world where people do terrible things. But as someone who had experienced trauma, she knew that doing this was more challenging and took more time than it often does for someone who hasn't experienced trauma.

If you have experienced trauma, know that there is hope and help available. The Resources section (page 145) contains more information on reaching out for help. There is also much to gain from the information and exercises in this book, which will support you in gaining more confidence in your ability to establish safety in your life. The following two exercises are especially useful if you have suffered trauma, but they can be practiced by anyone to help navigate anxiety, self-awareness, and boundaries.

FINDING CALM IN YOUR BREATH AND BODY

Engaging symptoms of trauma is best done in consultation with a therapist. But there are exercises that a person who has experienced trauma and who is interested in boundary-setting can try on their own. They almost all involve returning to a rich sensory experience anchored in the experience of your own body. Here is one to try when you notice that your nervous system is overly aroused (including accelerated heart rate, shallow breathing, erratic thoughts, and muscle tension):

1. Move deliberately and slowly into a comfortable seated position. See how slowly you can do it. Your slowness will not only calm your system, it will remind you also of your ability to govern your own body.

2. Cross your arms flat over your chest (your left fingertips touching your right shoulder; your right fingertips touching your left shoulder) and tuck your head so that your chin is closer to or touching your chest.

3. Continue to breathe in and out through your nose with slow breaths, especially making sure to exhale fully.

4. Lift your head and notice your environment. See if you can find three things of the same color. See if you can find three things of the same texture.

5. Now that you're oriented to your surroundings, settle your gaze on something beautiful and hold it there. A steady gaze can help promote a steadier mind.

6. Stay in this posture, continuing to breathe slowly and steadily, for as long as it feels soothing.

7. As you emerge from this posture, engage with someone in your support circle who promotes your sense of well-being: a friend, partner, family member, therapist, or clergy member.

By intentionally moving through this exercise, you are gently but firmly returning to a state in which you're reminded that your experience is anchored in your own body and breath, and that you can make choices that will help you return to a calmer state.

INNER AWARENESS AND HEALING

Peter Levine, author of *Waking the Tiger: Healing Trauma*, is an expert on trauma care. This exercise is adapted from an exercise he developed. Because trauma can result from a violation of the body or the self, a person living with the effects of trauma can experience some disconnection from the direct experience of living in their own body and perceiving their environment factually through their senses. Instead, they can live through the looping agitation of vigilance, as memories from the past and fears of the future cloud over contact with the present. In light of that disconnection, healing can take the form of "coming back into" their own body and their own senses of how things actually are. This can provide grounding and clarity to more easily and effectively practice healthy boundaries. The following practice can help encourage that subtle, but profound, shift:

1. Get into a comfortable position, lying down or seated, with your eyes open or closed.

2. With your palm flat, place your left hand on your forehead.

3. Now with your palm flat, place your right hand on your heart.

4. Continue to hold your comfortable posture, breathing in a regular and steady way, with your hands in those positions.

5. Levine recommends that you wait for a shift. The shift will be something inward, toward greater soothing. It's not a cathartic moment in which great truths are revealed; it's an awareness that greater peace has settled over you. When you feel that shift, move your left hand that has been on your forehead down to your belly (keeping your right hand on your heart). Hold it there.

6. Again, maintaining your comfortable posture, wait until you feel what you recognize as a shift. If the shift doesn't come, or at least in the way you expect, that's okay—you can practice again later.

Thought Patterns

A therapy client of mine, Tariq, was musically talented and had won special recognition at his conservatory 10 years ago, but he had not progressed in his career beyond that. When his professors encouraged him to enter competitions or to audition for particular roles, he would find a way to wriggle out of it. "Probably won't work out" was his mumbled refrain. Not surprisingly, Tariq's negative thought patterns helped protect him from the anxiety and risk of potential rejection. If he never went to an audition, he'd never have to suffer the pain of rejection. However, avoiding his vocation and his identity as a musician produced its own quiet suffering.

Maladaptive thinking patterns can be like Tariq's, protecting us in the short term and on the surface from harm, but also, perversely, creating longer-term damage by keeping us from the flourishing life we could have. Such thinking patterns include:

◆ Blaming others
◆ Making excuses instead of engaging with reality
◆ Depending on overly optimistic views that exclude awareness of difficulty or suffering
◆ Catastrophizing, blowing manageable situations out of proportion
◆ Seeing everything as either/or
◆ Not allowing ambiguity
◆ Jumping to conclusions based on assumptions, rather than waiting for evidence

Each of these patterns, different as they may seem, is a form of fantasy, a story that imagines the world in simple, black-and-white terms. Although it may seem strange that someone would choose, however unconsciously, to live in a fantasy (especially one that does not bring happiness), we can understand it as preferable to the complexity and ambiguity of life as it is. In Tariq's case, it was easier or safer to tell himself the story "It probably won't work out" than to engage with a life where things sometimes work out and sometimes don't. We can think of unhealthy thought patterns as anxiety-management systems that give us the pretense of certainty.

When you are working toward setting boundaries, you will almost inevitably need to overcome some degree of unhealthy thought patterns. As you do, you'll need to decide to live in the world as it is, full of complexity and contradictions, rather than the simplicity that unhealthy thought patterns provide.

CHALLENGING NEGATIVE THOUGHTS

Choose one of your negative thought patterns—for instance, a tendency to blame others for what's wrong. Now, think of the positive thought pattern you'd like to replace that negative thought pattern with. For instance, instead of blaming others, maybe you'd rather have the response that says, "Let me understand what happened factually, and then learn what I can do differently going forward."

This exercise asks you to focus on that desired replacement thought. In the table that follows each day you're invited to notice when that negative thought arises and what triggered it. Be gentle with yourself. Each of us has countless thoughts every day! So just pick one negative thought. Then, in the next column, write down how you challenged that negative thought. It's okay if you didn't challenge the negative thought immediately, in the moment. You can write down how you would have challenged the negative thought, replacing it with another perspective. Finally, write down what happened when you challenged the thought with a different response. What changed?

	WHEN THE NEGATIVE THOUGHT AROSE	HOW I CHALLENGED THE NEGATIVE THOUGHT	THE OUTCOME
Day 1			
Day 2			
Day 3			
Day 4			
Day 5			
Day 6			
Day 7			

FLIPPING THE SCRIPT OF YOUR "SHOULD"S

The word "should" sounds so authoritative because it's so judgmental. In fact, it's an irresponsible word, scolding us for our shortcomings without proposing a path forward. This exercise invites you to reframe the scolding, useless "should" with the more focused and constructive approach of experiments. For the "should" in your negative thought patterns, decide what experiment will take its place. It's true that finding a way to build habits is what really locks in desired behaviors. But for now, be gentle with yourself. Just try an experiment. You can always go back to the "should"s later, if you choose!

Whereas "should" is usually vague and general, experiments can be expressed in specific terms. So be specific about what you will do, when, and how long the experiment will last.

For example, you can reframe "I should get eight hours of sleep!" as "This week, I'll experiment with going to bed by 10 p.m." Or "I should eat healthier food!" can become "When I next go grocery shopping, I'll experiment by purchasing three vegetables I think I might like and looking up recipes to make them delicious."

YOUR "SHOULD" STATEMENTS	YOUR "EXPERIMENT" STATEMENTS
I should:	I will experiment by:
I should:	I will experiment by:

Continued ➤

Continued ➤

YOUR "SHOULD" STATEMENTS	YOUR "EXPERIMENT" STATEMENTS
I should:	I will experiment by:
I should:	I will experiment by:
I should:	I will experiment by:

Your Rights

Sarah's mother was well known in town for hosting fundraising events. But Sarah, at age 30, felt like Cinderella. Almost every weekend she'd be out at grocery stores, filling her cart and then hurrying back home to bake pastry puffs before racing to her mother's house to help serve, then clean up. Sarah resented it. It was only in group therapy that she realized how many rights she had given up: The right to say "no." The right, when her mother gave her a list of 10 things to do, to respond, "Here are the three things I'm willing to do," without explanation. The right to make her needs as much, if not more, of a priority than the needs of her mother. The right to pursue her own happiness. The right to decide how to spend her time.

The ethical life is always a balance of rights and responsibilities. Someone who's lived for years oriented to the needs of others will be more oriented to responsibilities. Rights, to such a person, may seem selfish. But exercising your rights means being responsible to, and for, yourself. Failing to exercise those rights is to be irresponsible to yourself.

The first step in establishing your rights is to identify them. Although there are ways that your rights are universal—the right to self-determination, for example—identifying and articulating your rights for yourself, in your own language, is essential. Naming is the first step in commitment.

After identifying your rights, it's important to reflect on where and when you'll exercise them, and to anticipate where and how resistance will arise. Resistance to exercising your rights may come from someone else, but it will also likely come from you. As with any exercise, strength and skill in exercising your rights comes from practice over time.

BOUNDARIES IN PRACTICE

Mariah and her friends were planning a camping trip. Her friends wanted to stay in the woods for three nights, but Mariah knew that would be too much for her—she was an introvert, after all. She let them know she'd camp for two nights. Immediately, her friends tried to change her mind. Mariah thought about explaining. She thought about making up an excuse. But then she remembered she didn't owe anyone an explanation. Her boundary was her boundary. She said, "I'm only going to camp for two nights. That's my decision." And that was that. When you set a boundary, you don't need to explain.

YOUR BILL OF RIGHTS

Writing the United States Constitution was an often-contentious process, a clash among patriots with different political philosophies. In the end, one of their solutions was to write a set of 10 amendments forever guaranteeing certain rights to the citizens of the new country. These are known today as the Bill of Rights. They include the freedom of speech, religion, and assembly.

As you think about your efforts to create clearer, stronger boundaries in the face of emotional hurricanes and the demands of others, what are 10 statements of inviolable rights that you can write down? For instance, for *How I express my feelings*, you might declare, *I have a right to express authentic anger*. For *How I make decisions*, you might declare, *I have a right to take all the time I need to make a thoughtful decision*. Make the statements clear and unwavering. Look at the following prompts to start to create your own Bill of Rights.

1. How I express my feelings: _____

2. How I protect my health: _____

3. How I make decisions: _____

4. How I use my time: _____

5. How I am treated by others: _____

6. How I spend my money: _____

7. How I engage with social media: _____

8. How I express my spirituality or greater purpose:

_____

9. How I relate to my family: _____

10. How I honor my body: _____

Your Values

Once, during a summer Army Reserve training session, my unit did a values-clarification exercise. After answering 200 questions and receiving an assessment, we were asked to find others who shared our values. I walked around looking for others who also had the values of "creativity," "curiosity," and "humor," but most of the other people in the unit had values such as "honor," "loyalty," and "service." I got some good-natured teasing! But the instructor was kind, telling us that diversity in values would strengthen us as a unit.

Personal values are ideals we intend to embody in our lives. They're important because they represent something about who we are. For instance, if someone grew up in an especially volatile household, as an adult they might hold as a value the importance of being peaceable with others.

Sometimes it's challenging to articulate your core values. On the one hand, they may be so much a part of the fabric of your life that you hardly notice them. On the other, they may seem so unattainable that it's hard to think about them without embarrassment. Try the following exercise to identify some of your core values.

WHAT ARE YOUR CORE VALUES?

Let's examine some positive values that have formed from your experiences in life. Think of times when you were especially proud of having lived as you intend to, even when it was hard. What were you doing? Why was that important to you? For instance, if you dropped out of college earlier in life and then went back to complete a degree, it might be important to you because it demonstrated persistence. From this experience, "persistence" might be a value. Or maybe you told your boss to stop harassing a coworker, which is important to you because you were brave; so "bravery" might be a value.

See if you can come up with five examples, using the table on page 46. In the left column, summarize each experience you're proud of. In the next column, say why it was important (you can start with *Because . . .*). Next, see if you can boil down why it was important to one or two words that describe an important value. Finally, look at all five values and assign them a rank, 1 to 5, based on their importance to you. In the next exercise, you'll reflect more on your top three.

YOUR EXPERIENCE AND WHY IT WAS IMPORTANT	NAME THE VALUE	RANK

HOW OTHERS RESPECT YOUR VALUES

Now that you've identified your top three core values, let's take a closer look. In the table on page 48, write down these values in the left column. Then do some thinking about each. As they relate to each value, write down the behaviors from others that you will allow, that you'll put up with (even if it's not your preference), and that you won't allow. For instance, using the previous example, if you identified "persistence" as a value that was important to you, under "Will Allow," you might write "teasing from my brother, because I know he's proud of me." Under "Will Put Up With," you might write "coworkers questioning my decisions at least a couple of times (but not constantly); it's irritating, but I know they're interested and a little envious." Under "Won't Allow," you might write "my mother criticizing my decisions and the habits of persistence I live by." If "respect" is a value, you may be willing to put up with someone inadvertently offending you, if they were willing to talk about it and agree not to offend you again, but you may not allow someone to blatantly disrespect you or others. If you have a particular context in mind—the workplace, your neighborhood, and so forth—it helps to get really specific, so you can have a very clear intention.

VALUE	WILL ALLOW	WILL PUT UP WITH	WON'T ALLOW

SHARING YOUR VALUES

Pick one of your core values. Invite someone important to you to share a structured conversation about a value that's important to you. Tell them the conversation is part of the personal work you're doing. Before you meet, think of three stories from your life that illustrate when that value has mattered, because of its presence or because of its absence. Open the conversation by spending a few minutes talking about the value you have chosen. Tell your conversation partner the stories you thought of. As you do, explain why those stories are important: what they mean to you, and how they shape your life. Next, share how you want your life to look as that value becomes more central for you.

Then ask the person about their relationship to the value you've discussed. Is it important to them? Can they share stories of their own? Listen and reflect. Then ask the person to give you feedback: When have they noticed you especially committed to that value? Please note, this is not asking them to tell you when you've fallen short. You're not inviting criticism. Finally, thank them for engaging with you. Invite them to support you as you make this value more central in your life.

Sometimes, asserting our values is a challenge; there can be pressure to keep quiet or trade away what we believe in just to conform to the expectations of others. Practicing talking about what's important to us can help us become more comfortable living authentically, according to what we believe. Inviting someone else to share what's important to them also helps teach us to be mindful of the beliefs that others hold. Practicing sharing what's important, especially in a relationship that's meaningful, can bring about a shift from relating to one another based on the pressures of conformity to relating to one another based on your authentic, solid selves.

Your Goals

When you take your last breath, what do you want to be true about your life? Some people set goals related to accomplishment: to visit every national park or to write a novel. Some have goals about getting good at something: juggling, public speaking, or knitting. For others, the goals are about the kind of person they want to become: generous, wise, or assertive. People set goals in the context of work, in the context of family, or just for themselves. Think about the goals you have for yourself. What do you want to accomplish, improve, or become?

To accomplish any of your major goals will require tenacious stewardship of your boundaries. You may have heard the phrase "No good deed goes unpunished." Well, it's also true that no audacious goal is pursued without tremendous resistance. To pursue a goal is, by definition, to pursue something different from the way things are now. Any kind of change that disrupts the status quo in our life patterns or relationships predictably invites a backlash. A spouse may be cranky that you're spending so much time training for that half-marathon when you used to enjoy leisurely Saturday mornings. A friend may feel abandoned now that you're finally working on that long-delayed novel. So serious pursuit of a goal requires you to anticipate what boundaries will need to be defended.

Goals can help clarify your boundaries, as well. When you are clear on the two or three things in life that you are prioritizing, at least for now, you are better able to see other things in proportion. For instance, if you have a goal to finish knitting a sweater by Christmas, then the boundaries on your time and other commitments will become clearer. The goal may mean saying "no" to helping out at the winter craft fair. Clear goals and boundaries give life a clear shape.

GOALS AND BOUNDARIES

Think of a goal you'd like to achieve. It could be a professional goal, a financial goal, a health goal, a relationship goal, or anything you choose that's important to you. Write it down.

....

....

Between you and the achievement of this important goal, there are obstacles and distractions. The obstacles are things you'll need to figure out and work through; they're the necessary problems to be resolved and overcome as you make your way toward the goal. The distractions, though, are things that take your attention from what you've said is important to you: your goal. These distractions will be seductive, because they'll occupy your attention with lesser concerns.

First, write down what your goal is.

....

....

Now, write down why it is important to you and how achieving it will benefit you.

....

....

....

Finally, in the table, write down the distractions and obstacles you can expect that will try to lead you away from your focus on the goal, and how you can use boundaries to navigate them.

DISTRACTIONS		OBSTACLES	
What distractions from pursuing your goal do you foresee?	For each distraction, what is a boundary you can set?	What obstacles to the goal do you foresee?	For each obstacle, what strengths will you bring to meet it?

PROTECTING THE TREASURE

If your goals are a precious treasure, your boundaries are the fortress walls that protect them. In the innermost circle here, write down your greatest goal (you can list more than one if you wish). Then, in the space outside both the circles, write down anything that could sabotage your goals, such as temptations, competing demands, guilty obligations, or whatever might threaten your intention to prioritize your own goals.

Finally, look at the band between those spaces. Think of this as the walls of the fortress, standing between your precious goals and whatever would threaten them. This is where you write down your boundaries. Be thoughtful in selecting your boundaries, considering each threat and what boundary will dissolve it or render it powerless.

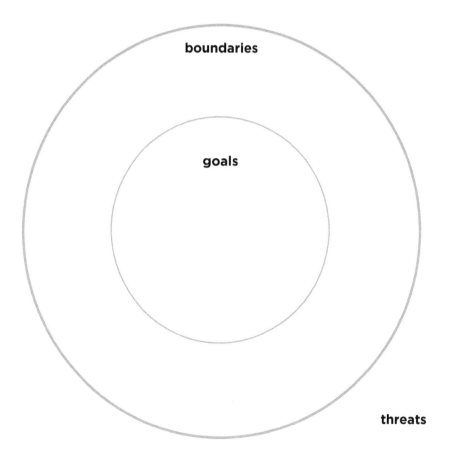

Key Takeaways

So many variables go into our boundaries: some from how life has shaped us and some from how we choose to shape life. Here are some central ideas we've covered in this chapter:

1. Each of us is shaped by powerful forces that affect our boundaries. Consider which, for you, are strongest.

2. Heritage and culture provide norms we may not be aware of, because they're so familiar. What does it take to become conscious of them and make choices about how we do or don't incorporate these norms into our lives?

3. People who've experienced trauma may, understandably, have self-protective but rigid boundaries. Boundary work may focus on the most basic level: helping heal the body.

4. Negative thought patterns need to be interrupted before their influence shapes our behavior more than our intentional boundaries would.

5. We each can establish our own Bill of Rights to clarify boundaries against external pressures.

6. Pursuing clear goals will help us keep our boundaries, and clear boundaries will help us pursue our goals.

CHAPTER 4

Setting Your Boundaries

In theory, boundaries seem like a good idea. They enable you to live with purpose, clarity, and power over your choices. What's not to like? But when you move from thinking to acting, things get trickier. As you bring boundaries into your life, you can expect resistance from others. It's not that other people don't want your well-being, it's that you're part of an intense relationship system. Your own efforts to change might provoke anxiety in others because it challenges them to change. This chapter will help you address those challenges so you can begin putting healthier boundaries into practice.

Setting Boundaries in a Family

From the start, babies are intensely oriented toward their primary caregivers. It's part of normal human development. Those relationships are how a baby regulates their sense of threat or well-being. As a child grows and becomes more functionally independent, emotional relationships with family can still be woven tightly. In many families, love is conflated with unwritten rules such as "Don't make Mom unhappy," "Don't tell our secrets," or "Pretend everything is okay even when it's not." All these rules have the same goal: to keep things calm and not upset the system.

But these rules can come at a high cost. They may hold family members hostage, not allowing them to grow or to make choices that would threaten the peace. Boundaries are about establishing independent selfhood. They're about saying "Here's what's mine and what's not mine." Ironically, that may be hardest to do among those who know and love you best. That's why it's so important!

Common Tensions with Children

There we are, at the grocery store, standing behind a mom with an overfilled shopping cart who's stretched thin, exhausted, and being pestered by her kids. One of them wants some candy. That kid is wailing and whining, and the mom is saying "no" but also looking around, embarrassed by what others might be thinking. She knows the family rule is no candy before dinner. She knows she's told her kid "no" and that changing her mind now will only reward the whining. But her kid is being so loud! So she relents. "Go ahead," she mutters as the kid tosses the candy into the cart.

Whether it's boundaries around screen time, eating, bedtime, or unruly behavior, parents can expect one guarantee for the limits they set: Their kids will test them. That's part of growing up—to learn how to live within boundaries and to negotiate them with others. Kids, especially under age 12, don't yet have the brain development to understand complex situations that require nuanced boundaries, so we can understand their rigid or rule-based view of the world. But we can also empathize with the mom: Sometimes we just want the whining to stop. In this section, you can try some exercises related to parenting boundaries. If you're not a parent, this section could be useful if you want to better understand others in your life who are parents. It can also be a way to take a different perspective on the parenting you, yourself, received growing up.

PARENTING CHECK-IN

Start by assessing how well you currently set boundaries with your children. Just decide whether each statement is true or false, circle your response, and see what becomes clear.

1. As a parent, thinking of my child's overall thriving, I'm clear about what's not my responsibility.   True   False

2. When my child's behavior leads to natural consequences—for instance, if they lose something it means they don't have that thing—I am comfortable allowing them to experience the consequences.   True   False

3. In parenting, I easily accept what I cannot control.   True   False

4. As a parent, I have disappointed my child with a clear "no" in the past week.   True   False

5. When my child is angry with me, I'm able to hear it while remaining relatively calm myself.   True   False

6. I'm able to stick to my parenting goals and values without much trouble.   True   False

7. If someone asked my children to tell them about the boundaries in our household, my children would be able to name them, even if they don't like them.   True   False

8. More or less, I'm parenting the way I intend to.   True   False

9. When I struggle in dealing with my children's behavior, I'm able to pause and collect myself so I don't lash out.   True   False

10. I ask my children to take responsibility for things in an age-appropriate way—neither too much nor too little.   True   False

How did you do? If you answered mostly "true," then you likely have a head start when it comes to setting clear boundaries with your children. If you answered mostly "false," like so many parents you may struggle to think and act clearly in moments of high emotion (and parenting is nothing if not emotional). Be gentle with yourself. No matter your situation, the following exercise will help you clarify some opportunities for growth in your parenting.

AREAS FOR IMPROVEMENT

Fill in the blanks in the following sentences to get some clarity on an area of tension for you. The sentences follow along in a sequence, one after the other, all addressing the same situation you identify in statement 1. You can use this exercise for different things you're working on, as long as all six statements are about the same topic each time you do the exercise.

1. I regularly get irritated when my child(ren):

_____

_____

_____

2. In response to this irritating behavior, I know it doesn't work in response when I:

_____

_____

_____

3. Another thing that doesn't work, which I've tried, is:

_____

_____

_____

4. As it turns out, I have a dilemma about responding to it. My dilemma is that, on the one hand, ..., and on the other hand, ...

5. How I respond to this behavior is important to me, because no matter what anyone else does, it's important to me that I always embody and express the value of:

....

....

6. Anchored in that value, in response to this irritating behavior, in the next week I will try a new kind of response. Instead of my old responses, which haven't worked, I will:

....

....

....

Common Tensions with Parents

"I told my mother not to give the children toy guns for Christmas," a client once told me. "And you know what she did? She gave them toy guns for Christmas! Well, I couldn't disappoint the kids, so I let them have the guns after all. But I gave my mother a piece of my mind, and she acted like she didn't know what I was talking about. This happens all the time."

It can be such a challenge to set boundaries with family. The intimacy and history of the relationships can heighten the anxiety and confusion involved.

According to *Family Estrangement: A Matter of Perspective*, by Kylie Agllias, 1 in 12 people are estranged from at least one family member. Often, this happens between adult children and their parents, when the choice seems to be between either fusing together as a part of a suffocating (and maddening) boundaryless closeness, or cutting off contact.

For people facing that either/or dilemma, neither option may be satisfactory. Thinking through and enforcing some clear boundaries can be a third option, a middle path between boundaryless fusion and outright estrangement.

YOUR RELATIONSHIP WITH YOUR PARENTS

Your relationship with your parents is often complicated and charged with unre-solved questions and tensions. This exercise is a guided writing prompt about that relationship that's intended to clarify your thinking and perspective about this important relationship. Working toward clarity can produce a shift, at least, if not resolution. Try to make each answer no more than 10 words. Limiting your word counts in this kind of exercise can prompt crisper thinking. Try it out.

1. Choose one of your parents. What's something you genuinely respect and appreciate about that person?

_____

_____

2. Describe some area of tension with that parent.

_____

_____

3. What does the parent do to contribute to the tension?

_____

_____

4. What is your contribution to the tension?

_____

_____

5. What has been the cost to you of living with that tension?

6. How is the tension you feel linked to your boundaries?

7. What would clear boundaries regarding your parent's behavior look like?

8. What stops you from setting clear boundaries about what you will and will not accept from your parent?

9. What would clear boundaries regarding your own behavior look like?

10. What stops you from setting clear boundaries about your own behavior?

THE 4-7-8 METHOD

Being able to set clear boundaries, especially in the context of challenging family relationships, requires the ability to regulate your anxiety. The clearest, most thoughtful boundaries are no good to you if, in the moment you must articulate them, you can't figure out how to calm that swirling storm of emotions inside. This exercise is for building your capacity to self-regulate. If you practice regularly, you will be able to access self-regulation (and the calm it produces) in a moment of escalated anxiety, when you want to be thoughtful and clear—for instance, in a moment when you are articulating a boundary. Derived from ancient yogic pranayama breathing exercises, the 4-7-8 method of self-soothing goes like this:

1. Sit somewhere comfortable with your back straight.

2. Exhale completely through your mouth.

3. Close your mouth and inhale through your nose for a count of four.

4. Now hold your breath as you count to seven.

5. Exhale completely, in a controlled way, as you count to eight.

6. This ends the first cycle. Repeat again at least three times.

As you complete this exercise, check in with yourself. How do you feel? You might feel calmer, more grounded. If you're still more rattled than you'd like to be, see if more cycles of this self-soothing exercise will help.

Common Tensions with Other Family Members

"Have you heard?" Eladia's aunt, Alma, loved to gossip, and now she had some fresh news. "Your mother's going to get a tattoo. You've got to do something about it! She'll be the laughingstock of the pool." Alma liked to spend summer days at the neighborhood pool with Eladia's mother. "You've got to stop her," Alma said. "Save her from herself!"

When Eladia hung up the phone, she was irritated. Alma had led similar campaigns against her, including trying to rally family members to convince her not to marry the man who was now her husband. But when she said anything, people would just chuckle, shrug, and say, "Well, that's Alma." Alma herself said, "Now, I know I can get a little nosy sometimes" like it was all a big joke.

Was Eladia overreacting? Family members can be notorious for getting in our business, trying to push their opinions and choices on us whenever we stray from the family script. Of course, they're acting out of their anxiety and "allergic reaction" to differences within the family. But if we're going to live the life we choose and not stay harnessed to people-pleasing, it's on us to set a boundary we mean to keep.

FAMILY GATHERINGS

Family get-togethers, or any encounter with a family member who oversteps your boundaries, can be a source of joy and meaning. But they can also be a source of high stress, as the familiarity and togetherness can run roughshod over your best intentions to maintain principled, well-defined boundaries. So let's reframe a family get-together as a chance to practice. Here is a checklist to consult before your next family gathering. Look it over and make sure you're ready by being able to check every item.

- ☐ I'm clear on my intentions for myself and my choices and behavior at this occasion.
- ☐ I know the boundary that will likely be tested.
- ☐ I'm aware of the moments in which I predict my anxiety will rise.
- ☐ I'm aware of the relationships that are likely to drive up my anxiety.
- ☐ I have a plan for how to rein it in when I start to become a little bit wobbly or jittery, driven more by anxiety than by clear thinking.
- ☐ I have a self-care/reset plan for what to do if I really start to get rattled.
- ☐ I have a plan to reflect afterward and celebrate how I did and what I learned.

A FRESH PERSPECTIVE

Sometimes tension with family feels deeply personal. That's understandable, given that it involves not only you but also the people who produced you. However, despite appearances, tension in families is usually not particular to one person or even one generation. Families develop certain patterns of relationships to collectively manage their otherwise unmanageable anxiety. Being trapped in those patterns can be uncomfortable.

One alternative is to develop some curiosity—to wonder, instead of fretting. Try this exercise to see how it works for you.

1. What is the relationship pattern that makes you uncomfortable?

....

....

2. Regarding the pattern, what information do you not know?

....

....

3. What's a question you could ask about what you don't know?

....

....

4. How could you find out information that would help you with that question?

....

....

5. Based on your new information, what's an experiment you could try to work on functioning differently when it comes to that uncomfortable pattern?

....

....

When you become curious about what annoys you, it can change your relationship to the annoyance. Seeing a wider pattern of behavior throughout the family system, across generations, can help you see the annoyance as impersonal, which can help you be more thoughtful about dealing with it, leading to a greater ability to set clear boundaries.

Boundaries with Romantic Partners

I once knew an elderly couple who'd squeeze in close at a breakfast diner and tell the waitress, "We take our coffee black." They did everything together. That intense togetherness can be hard to sustain, though. Even people who share a lot of the same interests may have different approaches to engaging with them. A relationship that requires partners to be joined at the hip is a relationship that manages a lot of pressure. Sometimes, people feel trapped, thinking it's either/or—joined at the hip or no relationship at all.

One common boundary issue in a relationship is related to socializing. Different people have different needs, values, and habits when it comes to socializing. One person may prefer to plan ahead; the other may like going out spontaneously. One person may simply prefer to socialize more than the other.

Couples need not attend every social engagement together. In fact, healthy couples often develop their own friendship networks, in addition to friendships both partners enjoy. Sometimes at weddings you'll hear a line about "two becoming one." But that's just not the case. Thriving couples remain two well-defined individuals who choose, every day, how they will show up for each other (and for themselves).

Common Tensions in Couples

Newly in love, it's hard for couples to imagine there could ever be trouble. "Finally, someone who really understands and respects me!" Buzzing with oxytocin—known as the "love hormone"—a new couple can glide fluidly through decision-making, compromising easily.

But infatuation lasts only so long. There soon comes a time when the ease of the early days can start to feel constraining, if not suffocating. Maybe at first it was a thrill to spend every spare moment together, but now you'd like to reclaim some time in your life for friends and hobbies—or just being alone.

Given the complexity of romantic relationships, couples can find themselves challenged by boundaries across a wide range of life: chores, finances, punctuality, sex, sharing personal information with family members, and so much more.

Some people in relationships hesitate to set boundaries. They fear it will hurt or even chase off their partner, as if the choice were between having a relationship or having personal boundaries. If they do set boundaries, they may struggle to maintain them; in the moment, it can seem easier to just go along with what their partner wants. But that short-term comfort often comes at the long-term cost of resentment.

It takes courage to articulate your boundaries with your partner, to assert your own needs and limits while also staying connected. It can take creativity as a couple to develop ways of sharing a life that honors the boundaries each of you has set. And, as with learning and practicing anything, incorporating boundaries into a relationship can take patience. But the reward is precious: a life in which both partners are honest and open, set free by their ability to trust that in this relationship living with personal integrity isn't just tolerated, it's celebrated.

It could be that you're currently not in a romantic relationship, but you have been in one before or would like to be in one. This section still applies to you. Take the opportunity to reflect on a previous relationship or to imagine the kind of relationship you'd like to have.

BOUNDARIES IN PRACTICE

Mei and Hyunju had been married 10 years, but even when they agreed on a monthly budget, Mei would overspend, sometimes by more than $1,000. Hyunju's problem wasn't how to get Mei to stop spending so much. It was how Hyunju could stop letting herself be trampled on financially. Ultimately, Hyunju decided to separate her finances from Mei's, even as they continued to happily enjoy marriage together. Now they'd each be responsible for their own part of their shared expenses. At first Mei was hurt by this decision, but in time she came to accept the need for it. Tensions around finances in the marriage began to subside as Mei gradually took more responsibility for her own spending.

In a relationship, boundary-setting isn't about how to change someone else. It's how to stop accepting the consequences of the other person's behavior on you.

HOW ARE THINGS GOING?

It's so important in a romantic relationship for each partner to continue to be clear with the other. This exercise invites you to do an inventory of how things are across different realms of a relationship, and to develop boundaries where they are needed. If you aren't in a relationship at the moment, you can use this exercise as a chance to reflect on a previous relationship.

	WHAT'S WORKING	WHAT'S NOT WORKING	BOUNDARIES THAT WOULD HELP
Communication			
Intimacy			
Finances			

Continued ➤

Continued ➤

	WHAT'S WORKING	WHAT'S NOT WORKING	BOUNDARIES THAT WOULD HELP
Commitment			
Dealing with conflict			
Decision-making			

BROACHING DIFFICULT TOPICS

When long-term couples become entrenched in old patterns, it can be hard for them to risk broaching certain topics and challenging certain long-standing agreements. Ironically, it's not always easy to break the ice with a longtime partner, to have a conversation that disrupts the status quo, such as one that sets new boundaries. If you're working up the nerve to have such a conversation, here are some steps to consider taking:

1. Think through what you want your partner to hear (which is different from what you want to say) and write it down.

2. Consider: When and where would be the setting for the most constructive conversation possible?

3. Is it better for your partner to know the topic of the conversation beforehand, because it will help them do some pre-thinking and they won't be surprised? Or is it better for them to know that this is going to be a meaningful conversation but not tell them the topic, because their anxiety would get the best of them? Record your thoughts.

4. How do you want to start the conversation? "You know, I've been think-ing" is a great way to start a conversation in which someone will introduce change to the other.

....

....

....

5. Can you say what you need simply, perhaps in three talking points? Once you have the statements, practice saying them out loud or while looking at a mirror, to become more comfortable expressing them.

....

....

....

GETTING CLEAR ON RELATIONSHIP BOUNDARIES

This fill-in-the-blanks exercise takes the previous exercise one step further, inviting you to focus on a particular area of tension in your relationship and the full process of enacting a boundary. Every relationship has areas of tension. Any relationship could use a tune-up; any partner can work to clarify boundar-ies that have become porous or murky.

1. In our relationship, one of the things that brings tension is:

....

....

2. In that area of our relationship, what happens is:

....

....

3. What I would like to happen instead is:

4. I know I can't change other people, including my partner, but because I can change myself, one life-promoting, self-loving thing I could do differently is:

5. To do that different thing consistently would mean holding a boundary; the boundary would look like:

6. This boundary would be important to me and our relationship because:

7. When I set that boundary, I can expect my partner to:

8. I might struggle to maintain that boundary because I myself might:

9. But I will dedicate myself to maintaining the boundary because I'm working toward a life that can be described by these words:

Boundaries with Friends

Danya saw her roommate, Tamika, across the courtyard. Tamika looked great—so full of energy and dressed really nicely as well. The way her red jacket set off her black pants was a great combination. But that jacket looked familiar. Danya stopped in her tracks. The jacket was hers! That night, Danya talked to Tamika about it. She didn't want Tamika borrowing things without asking. Danya had worked hard to buy herself some nice things. Tamika was surprised because she'd grown up with three sisters who always borrowed clothes from one another.

Early experiences that shape our assumptions and norms will affect our values and boundaries. Although family members and couples often have a clearer sense of mutual expectations, what's simply called "friendship" covers a much wider range of possible ways people relate to each other. My grandmother used the old-fashioned term "bosom friends" to describe people she had known almost 90 years. Others might hit it off with someone one night at a bar and call them a friend, too. When tension and difference arise in a friendship, it's especially important to explore what each person means by the word "friend," and even more important for each friend in a friendship to clarify their boundaries.

Common Tensions with Friends

Friendship, like any relationship, requires certain skills that take practice to build. One skill that supports friendship is upholding clear, consistent boundaries. Without boundaries, friendship can become yet one more stressor; people may drift even further from this source of meaning and support.

In a friendship, there are many common tensions that indicate where a person can set boundaries. Friends can find themselves competing with each other, romantically or professionally. Friends can have different ideas about what information is appropriate to share. Sometimes, one friend can pressure another for more frequent time together—to see each other once a week, say, instead of once a month. Or maybe a friend wants to drag their friend into activities that only one of them enjoys. Sometimes, a friendship becomes emotionally one-sided, as if it weren't a friendship but a free counseling service.

Friendship isn't easy. It takes showing up and practicing. And for friendship to last in a way that's satisfying to both, it takes setting clear boundaries.

FRIENDSHIP QUIZ

Take this True/False quiz to assess your current friendship practices. There is no grade or judgment. No one else needs to see your answers. It's only for you to see your own responses, to help you decide what changes, if any, you might make in the shape of your friendship boundaries.

1. The current number of friends I have is just right. True False

2. I see my friends as much as I want to—not too much nor too little. True False

3. When I am with my friends, we engage in activities that are meaningful to me. True False

4. When I am with my friends, I feel known and accepted for who I am. True False

5. I don't have any friends who intimidate or bully me. True False

6. In the past year, I have been able to successfully assert my own boundaries with a friend, even if it disappointed them. True False

7. I am currently in a friendship in which I'd like to set boundaries, but don't know how or have not yet. True False

8. I can trust my friends with sensitive information about myself.

True   False

9. I don't have any friends who pressure me to support them, emotionally or financially, in ways that are uncomfortable for me.

True   False

10. My friendships help me be more of the person I'm trying to become.

True   False

Now that you have taken this quiz, spend some time reflecting on what you learned. In particular, what's working well in your friendships? What's not working well? What would you like to change? This kind of reflection can help you put your observations into action.

A WEEK OF FRIENDSHIP

Especially in a century where the hours and energy given to work and parenting have sharply increased, and other hours can be consumed by the "snack food" social contact of social media, meaningful friendship can be a challenge to sustain. If other demands on your time mean you have not invested in friendship in the way that you'd like—that your weak boundaries around other things, perhaps, have allowed your intentions with friendship to fall away—this exercise may help. It's a week-long calendar, which you can reuse.

Take a few moments to think about what you'd like in your friendships, and then write down at least two actions you will commit to each day related to friendship. Don't let this feel overwhelming; think of it as a short experiment, just for a week. Examples of actions could be a phone call to a friend, sending a handwritten letter or card, or making a plan to see each other in person. It could even be a text, if that's an easy way to get started.

DAY	MY ACTIONS
1	
2	
3	
4	
5	
6	
7	

EXERCISE

In this exercise you will have a chance to examine a friendship in which you would like to have firmer boundaries.

1. Bring to mind a friend who oversteps your boundaries, knowingly or unknowingly. Now, consider what benefits have you gained from the friendship.

---

2. What do you wish you could receive from the friendship that you're not currently receiving?

---

3. What do you wish you could offer or share that you're not currently offering or sharing?

---

4. What's an important value to you that gets trampled or minimized in this friendship?

---

5. What boundaries would you like to set with that friend?

_____

_____

_____

6. How would you initiate a conversation to renegotiate boundaries? What do you expect the friend would do in response? How could you manage your emotions? (You may wish to reflect on the exercises you did in the previous chapter around regulating anxiety.)

_____

_____

_____

7. How would you stick to your boundaries while staying friends?

_____

_____

_____

Boundaries at Work

You may have heard the expression "working yourself to death." In the 21st century, the World Health Organization (WHO) reports that's increasingly the case. A study from the WHO and the International Labour Organization found that between the years 2000 and 2016, the number of deaths from heart disease related to working long hours increased by 42 percent and from stroke by 19 percent. As more and more is demanded, the compulsion to work without boundaries may seem overwhelming. We're facing longer hours, unexpected assignments, faster deadlines, and the dreaded "other duties as assigned," in which we're asked to do more than the job we agreed to. Against this rising tide, boundaries can form a seawall.

Common Tensions with Coworkers

Jayden worked for a tech company housed in a converted factory. The walls were exposed brick. The workstations were open tables set up here and there, interspersed with couches and armchairs. It was intended to encourage collaboration, but for Jayden it was a nightmare. Although gifted at their work, they struggled to concentrate in the presence of ambient noise. A coworker, Dan, often set up right near them. Dan loved to share the latest viral videos and recount hair-raising personal stories. Jayden often found themself scurrying around the office, carrying their laptop, trying to find a place to escape from Dan's eager friendliness.

Coworkers who share space often have boundary issues to work out with one another. Coworkers, like friends, can become competitive, creating an unsupportive environment with higher stress. Noise and interruptions are common. Because coworkers share the same mission but play different roles in that mission, they often need to make requests of one another. When and how it's okay to say "no" or to negotiate is a common area of boundary-setting.

As in any relationship system, coworkers can fall prey to gossip, another area where boundary-setting will help. And sometimes a coworker's personal need for control will turn into outright bullying, requiring a well-defined response that shuts that behavior down. The workplace is full of opportunities to practice boundary-setting.

A TIME-OUT MEDITATION

Especially when a coworker is getting on your nerves to the point where you're thinking about them often, fantasizing about showdowns or finally telling them off, the best first step is to dial down your anxiety a little so you can be more thoughtful about what you will do. When you're a little less reactive, you have more access to your capacity to think. This exercise is a body-scan meditation, letting you move from the grip of anxiety into the peace of your body.

1. Find a comfortable place to sit or even lie down. Close your eyes or focus on some still point in the room with your eyes half-closed.

2. Become aware of your breath moving in and out. Don't try to control it.

3. As you drop further into your body, notice somewhere on your body that is drawing your attention. You can move from toes to head, or head to toes, in order, if you like, or you can shift your attention to whichever place seems interesting to you right now.

4. Notice sensations in the part of the body you're attending to. There might be tingling or a twitch. There might be some pain. You might not be able to feel it at all. See what you notice—no judgment, no fixing.

5. Your attention will drift. That's normal and okay. Gently bring your attention back to the part of your body you want to observe. When you're done there, move to the next part of your body. Continue to breathe slowly and steadily.

6. When you've completed your observation of the various parts of your body, turn your attention to your whole body at once. Just notice. No judging. No fixing. Keep breathing.

7. Come to the end of this exercise. Return gently and mindfully to engagement with your day.

SETTING BOUNDARIES WITH A COWORKER

Having an irritating—or worse—coworker provides a good opportunity to set some boundaries. Once again, boundaries aren't just a good idea; they're a set of behaviors to put into practice to uphold your integrity.

Consider this experiment. Think of behaviors at work that violate your boundaries. Not behaviors you dislike or disapprove of; behaviors that cross your line. Using the chart on page 80, record the boundary-crossing behavior, your response, and your observation (what you notice or learn from recording the behavior and your response).

Be gentle with yourself. This is a learning process, not a get-it-right-the-first-time exercise. You're observing things about your own fears and motivations that might be obstacles to you establishing clearer boundaries. Keep going!

	YOUR COWORKER'S UNDESIRED BEHAVIOR	YOUR RESPONSE	YOUR OBSERVATION
Day 1			
Day 2			
Day 3			
Day 4			
Day 5			

Common Tensions with Your Boss

It was Saturday afternoon. Sandra, who worked Monday to Friday, was out with her friends when her phone buzzed. It was a text from Dr. Zee, her boss. "Are you busy?" it said. She didn't respond. Two minutes later, another one. "I could really use your help." Sandra worked at a social services agency that helped people experiencing homelessness. The mission was powerful. Dr. Zee's leadership was inspired. Sometimes too inspired. The guy worked seven days a week, and he expected everyone else to as well. When people set boundaries, he didn't get angry. He got disappointed. It was painful to be the subject of Dr. Zee's withering disappointment. Sandra sighed and let her friends know she needed to bail on their outing. "Again?" one of her friends asked.

A relationship with a boss can be complicated. A boss can be a mentor. A boss can be a taskmaster. A boss can be a gateway to opportunities. A boss often controls access to resources linked to our primal sense of survival—namely, our paycheck. Sometimes a relationship with a boss involves several of these things at the same time. When they make a request or give a direction, our response is informed not only by our own principles and clarity about our role, but also by awareness of these complicating factors. That creates a dilemma.

The mature resolution to this dilemma is to be neither abjectly obedient nor impulsively rebellious in your relationship with a boss, but to clarify boundaries that allow you to serve the mission of your work in a way that upholds your integrity.

THE WORKPLACE CULTURE

Sometimes, communities, families, or workplaces have damaged boundaries without anyone being aware of them, because they have become part of the culture. This assessment is a quick check of the culture around boundaries at your workplace. Answer these statements as true or false.

1. Every employee has a job description that accurately describes what they're expected to do.   True   False

2. Every employee receives periodic, scheduled evaluations. The basis of the evaluations is fair and transparent, and the consequences and support for improvement are proportional and fair.   True   False

3. Supervisors or people with more power in the work system don't leverage their power or relationships to pressure supervisees or people with less power.   True   False

4. Employees have a clear way to express a difference of opinion without being punished.   True   False

5. Employees have a clear, trusted way to express a grievance.   True   False

6. The organization does what it says it does; there is alignment between written policies and actual behavior.   True   False

7. Employees are not asked to sacrifice important personal commitments to fulfill their work.   True   False

8. Unreasonable demands are not made of employees.   True   False

If you answered mostly "true," then it's likely that your workplace feels safe and supportive. If you answered mostly "false," then it's likely that your workplace is a challenging place in which to set and keep boundaries. The next exercise provides a good starting point for focusing on a particular boundary you would like to set, and it can offer a template for others, too.

BETTER BOUNDARIES WITH YOUR BOSS

Use these writing prompts to clarify your thinking about your relationship with your boss:

1. What boundaries of yours are respected by your boss?

_____

_____

_____

2. How does your boss demonstrate that respect?

_____

_____

_____

3. What boundaries of yours are not respected by your boss?

_____

_____

_____

4. How does your boss demonstrate that lack of respect?

_____

_____

_____

5. If your boss respected those disrespected boundaries, what behavior would your boss demonstrate?

6. Looking at your part in the current dynamic, how could you begin to enact boundaries in the area you described in question 3?

7. If you enacted boundaries in that area, what response would you expect from your boss?

8. How would you handle the response you expect?

Boundaries with Yourself

Part of the human condition is that often a person will intend to do A but end up doing B. For instance, on Monday morning a person may intend to exercise every day, but when Saturday comes, realize that they only exercised once. Learning to govern ourselves isn't easy.

Especially when we seek to change our behavior, we can expect to encounter resistance—not only from others, but also from within ourselves. Change of any kind can be perceived as a threat to the familiarity, comfort, and security of established patterns of behavior. So as we seek some change in our lives, or as we seek to behave in ways we haven't before (whether with regard to exercise, assertiveness, or some other realm of life), it's normal for some resistance to come up from within, pressuring us to revert to our old ways. Clearer boundaries with ourselves aren't easy. But we need them in order to live the way we're intending to live.

Common Tensions with Yourself

The human brain—the one you're using to read this sentence—is the largest and most complex of any primate. Humans have developed the field of quantum mechanics, made great works of art, and pulled off the Yurchenko double pike, as gymnast Simone Biles did in 2021. Humans, in other words, are capable of brilliance.

Yet so often we fail to do what we intended to do. We find ourselves at the end of a day or a week having spent our time and our energies in ways other than we had planned. We meant to spend $100 at the grocery store but instead spent more than $200. We meant to get in 10,000 steps a day, but we spent most of the day sitting down. Some people struggle in other areas, too, unable to keep our own boundaries in relation to sexual activity or acting out in anger or staying connected to a relationship in the way we meant to.

Aligning our actions with our intentions isn't a matter of sheer willpower. Therapists often call that strategy "just white-knuckling it." Clarity about goals, about what we're really trying for, in our actions is essential. Sometimes, we adopt a goal because we feel we should, or because it's important to others. When we understand why a goal is important to us—when it makes sense within our larger view of our own life—then it truly becomes our own goal, not the pursuit of a goal being performed for judging bystanders. Moving down the road in that light, boundaries become the guardrails helping us stay in the lane we meant to travel down.

MAKING A VISION BOARD

Visualization is a powerful practice. When you spend time focusing on what you want in your life, you become more oriented to it and can better organize your behavior around it. One way to visualize is to make a vision board.

A vision board is a collection of images of what you want in your life. For this exercise, it helps to have poster board (or at least a very large sheet of paper), scissors, glue or clear tape, and some pictures (from a magazine or printed off the internet). Think broadly across life's different dimensions: your family, your friendships, your work, your creative life, your intellectual life, your health, your finances. Maybe printed images don't do it for you. That's okay! You can draw the pictures. If it helps, you can find examples of vision boards online, but be careful not to fall into the trap of trying to copy someone else's in format or content. This is *your* vision board. So have fun assembling it.

When you're finished, put it where you'll see it every day. Spend time with it. Meditate on it. Think about it. Then, when questions about boundaries come up, you'll have an answer to the question "Why this boundary?" Because boundaries help remove the obstacles to the things you really want, which is all those things on your vision board.

IMPROVING THE REALMS OF YOUR LIFE

This is an exercise in setting intentions in different realms of your life. Setting an intention is different from making a goal. It's broader and less action oriented. For example, *I will climb Mount Kilimanjaro in Tanzania before I turn 50* is a specific goal, whereas *I will lead a life of adventure* is a broad intention.

Although this exercise asks you to review and gain clarity on several dimensions of life, it's probably more effective, strategically, to choose one realm of life to focus on first. Sometimes when people get energized, they want to tackle everything all at once. This exercise is only to help you see the field of play in your life, to get a little clearer about where you could be more mindful. Then, when you take it all in, you can choose the area you'll start your boundary work on.

To do this exercise, in the Vision column write your vision for each particular realm of life. Then, beside it, write what actions you'll need to take to support that vision. Finally, write down any boundaries that will be important to set and maintain to help you take those actions.

For example, for mental health, *I can do hard things without being overwhelmed* might be your vision; *I average eight hours of sleep each night and I meet with a therapist at least once a month* might be the actions you take to support that vision; *I don't engage in relationships that belittle or humiliate me* might be a boundary you set to help you take those actions.

	VISION	ACTIONS	BOUNDARIES
Mental health			
Physical health			
Diet and exercise			
Sleep			
Professional			

Continued ➤

Continued ➤

	VISION	ACTIONS	BOUNDARIES
Creative			
Spiritual			

Key Takeaways

We've covered a lot in this chapter. To reinforce your learning and growth, take a moment to review these key takeaways:

1. Boundaries aren't just an idea. They require practice. In what area of your life right now do you think you've got the best opportunity to practice?

2. The emotional intensity of families can seem to melt whatever boundaries you intended to set. With whom in your family do you have the hardest time keeping boundaries?

3. Thriving romantic relationships include clear, consistent boundaries. Think about your own view of well-boundaried love.

4. Friendships are so varied. What are the various needs and boundaries you seek and set with your friends?

5. In the 21st century, the hours of our life engaged in work—and the stress related to overworking—have skyrocketed. Especially when it comes to financial insecurity, which is connected to our survival, it can be hard (but important) to set boundaries.

6. When trying to change or govern one's own behavior, the solution isn't always trying harder. It's often getting clearer.

CHAPTER 5

Communicating Your Boundaries

So far, we've covered what boundaries are and why they're important. We've explored how boundaries are not just ideas but also practices to work at and strengthen in the context of real life and relationships. We've worked on how to set boundaries in many areas of life.

Boundaries aren't just communicated through behavior. It's possible (sometimes even preferable) to articulate them directly to other people. "Possible," of course, does not mean easy. Many of us were taught to avoid conflict, to steer around touchy subjects, and to "make nice." As a result, we end up suffering in silence. So it's important to learn how to talk about boundaries. That's what this chapter is all about.

Communication Dos and Don'ts

As Thanksgiving approached, Casey got a knot in her stomach. It seemed like the same thing happened every year. She, her husband, Raj, and the kids would go over to her mother's house. Then her uncle Dave would arrive, along with seven or eight other relatives. At some point, Raj and Uncle Dave would start talking politics. The men's disagreements, fueled by alcohol, would devolve into a shouting match. Casey's mother would end up sobbing and incapacitated, and Casey would have to serve Thanksgiving dinner to everyone, resenting them all. Besides skipping the whole thing, what could she do?

Successful Communication

What would it look like for Casey to use healthy communication strategies to address this problem? Let's see:

Set up a conversation. First, in the weeks leading up to Thanksgiving, Casey sets up a one-on-one conversation with each of the people whose behavior brings her distress: her husband, her uncle, and her mother. Ideally, these conversations don't ambush the other person but are made as appointments for the explicit purpose of "discussing expectations for Thanksgiving." Knowing the topic will help the other person do some thinking beforehand.

Clearly explain boundaries. As each conversation begins, Casey assesses the situation: Is her conversation partner clearheaded, sober, focused, and able to fully take part? If so, she tells them exactly the behavior that she objects to. She describes it in a straightforward, factual, and unemotional way. She says that she has a right to enjoy Thanksgiving and that she's no longer willing to tolerate or cover up other people's behavior. So she wants to communicate what she will and won't tolerate at Thanksgiving, and how she intends to respond to behavior that she won't tolerate.

Language and posture. Throughout the conversation, she uses "I" language as much as possible. This is because she's taking responsibility for her own actions, not focusing on trying to change someone else. While she talks, she makes sure her body language matches her confident words.

Follow through. Casey tells her husband and her uncle that if they begin fighting, they'll need to go outside, out of earshot. If they don't, she says, she will go eat Thanksgiving dinner at a restaurant. She tells her mother simply that she is ready to support her mother in hosting Thanksgiving by setting the table, washing dishes, and helping in other ways. But she is no longer willing to completely take over hosting duties while her mother sits in the kitchen crying. If her mother falls apart, Casey will read a magazine on the couch until her mother resumes hosting, at which point Casey will support her again. If Uncle Dave gets defensive or belligerent in the boundary conversation, she'll just end it and try again when he can fully take part.

That is Casey's healthy boundaries communication. In the rest of this chapter, you'll learn how to put these steps into practice for yourself.

KNOWING WHAT TO SAY

Plan your own healthy boundary-setting conversation, responding to the prompts in this exercise.

1. With whom will you have a one-on-one boundary-setting conversation?

....

2. What is the behavior you will no longer tolerate?

....

3. What has been the impact of that behavior on you?

....

....

....

4. When that behavior arises again, how do you intend to respond?

....

....

....

5. What will support you in responding the way you intend to?

....

....

....

6. Where and when is the best setting to have your one-on-one boundary-setting conversation?

....

....

7. As you begin, how will you assess whether your conversation partner is ready to participate? What kind of response from your conversation partner are you curious about and open to receiving? What kind of response are you not open to receiving (for instance, insults or defensiveness)?

....

....

....

8. After the conversation, regardless of what happened, what will you do to assess how it went?

....

....

....

Unsuccessful Communication

We've seen what it looks like for Casey to address the Thanksgiving situation in a healthy manner. Now we'll use the same scenario to see what unhealthy and unsuccessful communication looks like over a span of a few years.

◆ In year one, Casey sighs loudly and rolls her eyes when her husband and her uncle start fighting.

◆ In year two, in the car on the way to her mother's house, she says to her husband sarcastically, "I sure hope you have some political opinions to share with Uncle Dave." She's similarly passive-aggressive with her mother and her uncle.

◆ In year three, she tries to bribe all three of them. She offers her husband his favorite breakfast the next day if he behaves at Thanksgiving. She tells her mother she'll clean the whole house if she can only hang in there. She tells her uncle Dave, who is unemployed, that she'll call the friend she knows who might be hiring, if he will behave. (This manipulation actually works that year, but then Casey finds she's only made things worse, because she's now responsible for thinking of prizes every year to get the behavior she wants. Some people use threats, but it's the same basic set-up where we take on responsibility for how other adults behave.)

◆ In year four, Casey decides she's had it. When the political talk starts, she starts screaming at all of them and throws a dish on the floor, breaking it. That certainly captures people's attention, but it's not exactly communicating a boundary. It's more like a tantrum.

Unhealthy and unsuccessful communication may ask other people to read our minds or respond to some pressure we have brought to bear, whether that's guilt, threats, or bribes. Another form of unsuccessful communication involves beating around the bush or speaking in generalities. For instance, Casey might say something like, "You know, family gatherings are so much nicer when everyone gets along." Speaking like that, she might also hunch over or avoid eye contact. She has said something true, but she hasn't really addressed the issue.

Ideally, healthy communication about boundaries is a dialogue in which both parties listen and learn. Unsuccessful communication involves less listening and no learning. The most common unsuccessful communication, however, is to remain silent. So even if you do it imperfectly, if you take the risk of communicating, that's a promising start.

CONSTRUCTIVE CONVERSATIONS

Nonviolent communication is a framework designed for effective conversations about difficult things. It follows four steps:

1. Observation: State the facts without judgment.

2. Feelings: Share what feelings you have about what you've observed.

3. Needs: Articulate what's at stake. Why does this matter to you?

4. Request: Ask for what you need.

For instance, if I saw a neighbor allowing his dog to go to the bathroom in my front yard, I'd say, "When I see you allowing your dog to make a mess where my kids play (observation), I feel upset (feelings), because it's important to me to live in a considerate neighborhood and I have a right to a clean yard (needs). Would you be willing to pick up your dog's mess from now on (request)?"

Now, bring to mind a boundary that you might normally find difficult to communicate with someone. Write down what you would say to express your observation, feelings, needs, and request to this person.

1. Observation: _____

2. Feelings: _____

3. Needs: _____

4. Request: _____

Creating Consequences

Katarina was exasperated. She had asked her kids countless times to please rinse their dishes after dinner and put them in the dishwasher. But here it was 10 o'clock on a weeknight and the sink was piled high with her kids' dishes. She realized that although she'd clearly expressed her request, she had not communicated a consequence.

As helpful as nonviolent communication can be in a dialogue, if this kind of conversation hasn't proven effective, it's time to set boundaries. And boundary violations need consequences. When creating consequences, it's important that they are proportional to the offense. For instance, for failure to rinse the dishes and put them in the dishwasher, Katarina could say her kids have to cook dinner for a week. This may or may not be proportional. Certainly, it would be disproportional if, for failure to rinse their dishes one night, she said they had to cook dinner for a year.

Consequences for boundary violations need to affect the violator and not the one who's been violated. For instance, if Katarina said that failure to rinse dishes meant they couldn't eat dinner together for a week, but eating together was meaningful to her, that consequence would punish her.

Finally, effective consequences need to be handled as calmly and reasonably as possible. This means informing the other party beforehand of the consequences and then implementing them with clarity and consistency when the offending behavior happens, without too much fuss. As you plan your boundary-setting conversation, try using the nonviolent communication from the previous exercise to organize your thoughts and give structure to your communication strategy, and replace the request with a statement of the consequences.

Katarina's parenting scenario is different from adult-to-adult boundaries. With other adults, we're not in a position of authority so we won't be able to withhold privileges or implement punishment. Instead, with a peer, a consequence will be to say something you will do or won't do as a result of their behavior. For instance, if someone told a racist joke at a party, I would not go to their parties anymore. Meaningful consequences are clear, thoughtful, proportionate, and followed in a disciplined, matter-of-fact fashion.

THE RIGHT CONSEQUENCES

We all know the story of Goldilocks and the Three Bears. When Goldilocks tastes the bears' porridge, the first bowl is too hot and the second too cool, but the third one is just right. As we strive to determine proportionate consequences to violations of our boundaries, we may need to do some thinking and experimenting as well. If we've been trampled on before, it may be because we didn't establish clear consequences for boundary violations. But we can swing too far over to the other side, too, with outrageous consequences that don't fit the "crime." This exercise invites you to think about a few examples of what kinds of consequences you might set, and whether they are appropriate.

Boundary Violation	Consequence That's Too Harsh	Consequence That's Too Mild	Consequence That's Just Right	Does the "Right" Consequence Fall on the Violator or the Violated?

SHIFTING RESPONSIBILITY

Suppose your spouse is using your special shampoo—the shampoo that you bought as a treat for yourself and that you have communicated is yours alone to use. (You're happy to share lots of other things, just not this special shampoo!) But your spouse keeps using it.

You could suffer in silence. You could blow up in exasperation. You could work hard to figure out what consequences are appropriate. But here's another option: Tell your spouse what you see happening, and that you believe part of the reason the problem keeps recurring is that they have no consequences for violating your boundary. Ask them what they think is an appropriate consequence.

Often in this kind of conversation, the person will try to argue that your boundaries are inappropriate or they will try to justify their transgression. You can stop them right there by holding up your hand. Redirect by saying, "I'm not debating my boundary. I'm clear on that. I'm asking about the consequences for when you violate my boundary." Inviting the other person to be responsible for coming up with their own consequence not only relieves you of more effort but also invites them to more thoughtfully engage with the problem they've created.

Use this space to write out the script for what you will say to someone about their boundary violation, using the sequence above (what you see happening, noting that there are no consequences, proposing they come up with their own consequences).

Handling Negative Reactions

When you set boundaries, it's not to gain the approval of someone else, and the boundaries apply regardless of whether that person will behave perfectly. You set boundaries because you're ready to claim your own space in the world, not because you're going to continue organizing your behavior around other people's approval or disapproval.

But if being sensitive to other people's reactions is what has given you trouble with boundaries in the first place—if it has often been more important in your life to protect yourself against the negative reactions of others than to protect your own agency or your own feelings—then you can expect it will take some time and practice to develop equanimity about others' negative responses to your clear boundaries.

A challenge to your assertion of your own boundaries can look different, depending on the person and the circumstances. Someone can test your limits, acting in ways that dance right up to the line. Or perhaps step over it quickly to see what you will do in response. Someone can outright push back, arguing against your boundaries. Or they can question you, as if it was their role to interrogate you on a decision you made about your own boundaries.

Some people are in love with their own sense of virtue and can't tolerate being told that they've behaved in unwanted ways. So they respond with defensiveness. A manipulative tactic is the silent treatment or other behavior that withholds love and connection in a bid to get you to relent and renounce the boundaries you've set.

You can expect all kinds of negative reactions when you clearly set boundaries. And you can lovingly see them as signs of anxiety in someone else, as they realize how serious you are about living in a new way.

BOUNDARIES IN PRACTICE

Julie had converted to Judaism but hadn't yet told her manager what that meant about her availability to work on Saturdays, given the Sabbath practice she had committed to. When she did tell him, he sneered, "Well, that's awfully convenient. A lot of people would like to take Saturdays off." She said, "I don't need you to approve of my religious choice. I need to know whether you'll take me off Saturday shifts. If you won't, I'll need to contact a lawyer to learn my options in response to workplace discrimination." When someone reacts negatively, we need not engage them or try to persuade them. We can simply state our boundary and the consequences for violations.

SELF-REGULATING EMOTIONS

After doing all the work to identify our boundaries, then acting on them and communicating them clearly to others, if we then have to be on the receiving end of someone else's negative reactions, it can feel defeating and deflating. Perhaps that's because part of us still believes that our boundaries need to be validated by others to be legitimate. They don't.

How can we come to peace with our own boundaries, even when others cannot? This is where working on self-regulation becomes so important. Self-regulation means relying on ourselves, not on external conditions or other people, to regulate our anxiety and calm. This, of course, is easier said than done.

Taking up some regular habit of meditation, yoga, or spiritual practice can really reset your default level of sensitivity and anxiety over time. But in the moment, it helps to have something simple. So here it is:

1. Sit in a comfortable position.

2. Exhale until you have emptied your lungs.

3. Breathe in, then again exhale until you have emptied your lungs. Try to do this for about two minutes.

4. When anxiety arises, notice the thought attached to it and let it pass like a leaf floating down a river.

5. When you find you're distracted, gently come back to this simple practice of completely emptying your lungs with each exhalation.

When you're upset, your breath will tend to become shallow. Mindfully making sure your exhales are long and full can help you come back to the calm—not only mentally, but also physiologically—that will help you face what you need to face.

FINDING A NEW BALANCE

We know that new boundaries upset the balance in a relationship system. Others may be surprised or even feel threatened by our boundaries and may respond negatively. We can empathize with their reactivity, seeing it as part of their process toward ultimately accepting the new state of things.

However, as part of our strength in upholding boundaries, we need not be sponges for the bad behavior of others, simply absorbing their anxiety. How can we tell the difference between empathy and capitulation? How can we be open, so that others can feel what they feel, without leaving ourselves unprotected or required to withstand unacceptable behavior? This simple chart exercise can help. Use the space to brainstorm what negative reactions you will and won't tolerate in response to boundaries you set.

I WILL TOLERATE	I WILL NOT TOLERATE

Now, do some brainstorming about your responses. Make a list of possible responses you could have when someone does something you will not tolerate. For instance, a playful, lighthearted example could be, with a wink, "Excuse me, could you try saying that again?"

Respecting Other People's Boundaries

Throughout this book, we've discussed the importance of focusing on your own needs and your own boundaries. But as you grow in self-respect, you'll notice that your desire and ability to respect others grows, too. Likewise, as you grow in your capacity to define your own boundaries, you'll likely find that you're more aware of the boundaries of others, and that you want to respect them, knowing how important they are. Because boundaries are engaged most often in the context of relationships, at its best, boundary-keeping can be lovingly mutual, each of us honoring and protecting the other's boundaries.

Look for Cues

Research shows that most of us think highly of ourselves. Even those who can be self-critical about specific faults tend to believe they are morally superior to others. It's called the "self-enhancement effect." This perspective goes hand in hand with confirmation bias, which is where we seek evidence that supports our current views and don't notice anything that contradicts them. Together, these two human tendencies put us at risk of being insensitive or just plain clueless. If we're not careful, without realizing it, we'll trample someone else's boundaries.

As we've discussed, boundaries are personal, specific, and sometimes depend on context. How on earth are we supposed to keep track of other people's boundaries when we may be struggling to keep up our own? Of course, when in doubt, it's always okay to ask directly; most often, people will take that as a sign of care and respect.

We can also read cues to see if we've made a misstep. For instance, someone might avoid eye contact with us; that's a cue that something might be amiss or worth checking in on. They might back up, fold their arms, or make nervous gestures. A person might make a very limited response, like a grunt or a shrug. We can resist noticing, but if we're mindful, we'll read the cues and adapt our own behavior.

BOUNDARIES IN PRACTICE

For three days, Sunita hadn't returned Helen's texts. Helen wondered if Sunita was sick and brought her some homemade bread. But Sunita was standoffish, receiving it on the porch, avoiding eye contact. Helen said, "Okay, what's wrong?" Sunita paused, then burst out, "When you were at my house, you drank the last ginger ale! I'd been saving it!" They both burst out laughing and hugged. Helen apologized for being thoughtless, taking a drink from the refrigerator without asking. Sunita said she'd be more direct in the future. Checking in with a friend directly can bear the fruits of forgiveness and reconciliation.

ENGAGING WITH OTHERS

Think of someone in your life who struggles with boundary-keeping, perhaps especially in their relationship with you. This could be a family member, a spouse or partner, a child, or a friend. This exercise is about becoming a better detective, learning to notice the nonverbal signs of their discomfort when they're working on something they haven't quite worked out yet.

Here's something great: You don't need to keep it a secret, trying to catch them making nonverbal cues. You can say, "Hey! I want to support your boundaries better. One way I can do that is by noticing when I've screwed up and violated your boundaries. I know you can sometimes have a hard time telling people directly what's bothering you. So let's brainstorm together." Often, people will know exactly what their own bag of tricks is. Other times, people may not be so sure. So you can discuss, or agree to notice together going forward.

Use this exercise to think through a relationship you'd like to improve by better respecting someone else's boundaries. Respond to the prompts as a way to prepare for actually engaging someone important in your life.

1. Who is the person you'd like to engage?

2. What boundary do you suspect they let you violate?

3. When will you engage with them about this?

4. What's an opening line for what you will say?

5. How will you know they truly want to engage in this conversation and aren't just appeasing you?

Manage Your Reactions

You know how other people can have negative reactions to our boundaries? Well, it turns out that we ourselves can also have less than understanding and open-minded responses to the boundaries of others. If someone's boundaries make us twitch, or make us mad or defensive, it doesn't mean we're bad or cruel. It does mean it's time to slow our reactions and get curious. When our anxiety rises, it's because something within us feels threatened. Curiosity can help us figure out what that is.

For instance, I used to visit Atlanta twice a year. On the day I arrived, I'd call up old friends to see who wanted to get coffee or lunch. Finally, one friend, Dan, said, "Man, I love to see you, but life is busy. Give me a week's notice and we'll make plans." I had to figure out my negative reaction to that reasonable boundary. It turned out that my last-minute calls were connected to my own sense of improvisation and adventure that I liked to have when I went to Atlanta. I had to identify it to be able to renegotiate it within myself and see that it was easy to respect Dan's boundary.

A DIFFERENT ANGLE

When someone else's boundary has you upset, you may be inclined to focus on your own perspective and your judgment of their boundary. It can be helpful to try to shift to a different angle. A different angle doesn't dismiss the hurt you feel or the judgment you have; it just invites you to consider another way to see things. That's what this exercise is for. Bring to mind a situation, real or imagined, in which another person's boundary upset you, and complete the sentence:

1. The boundary that this person is holding is:

....

....

2. They have communicated the boundary to me by:

....

....

3. In response to that boundary, I feel:

4. The boundary changes our relationship in a way I don't like because:

5. A question I could ask this person is:

6. A question I could ask myself about this is:

7. What I will do in response to this boundary is:

8. I will respond that way because what's important to me is:

Key Takeaways

In this chapter we've moved from exploring the nature of boundaries to the practical art of communicating and enforcing them. Here are some central ideas from this chapter:

1. As well as identifying boundaries and practicing them, it's also important to successfully communicate the boundaries with significant others in your life.

2. Successful communication is direct, uses "I" statements, and communicates consequences for violations. Unsuccessful communication is passive and relies on mind reading, or it's passive-aggressive, manipulative, or aggressive.

3. Boundaries without consequences for violations aren't functioning boundaries; they're only ideas. Consequences should fall on the violator, not the violated.

4. Boundary-setting can be expected to provoke negative reactions from others who may feel threatened by a shift in the relationship. You can decide which reactions you'll allow and which you won't.

5. As you set your own boundaries, you'll increasingly recognize and honor boundaries in others. When you live a well-defined life, you appreciate clear boundaries in the lives of others, as well.

6. When you struggle to accept someone else's boundaries, it's a chance to get curious about what within you feels threatened.

CHAPTER 6

Practicing Self-Care

There's logic to boundarylessness. At some point early on, asserting clear boundaries would not have been safe. Maybe it was at home, maybe it was out in the world, but somewhere, somehow, pleasing or soothing other people became an effective strategy for staying safe. Consequently, asserting boundaries as an adult can feel risky, even dangerous. We may work up the nerve to assert a boundary on one occasion, only to anxiously let it collapse the next time.

Be gentle with yourself. Boundaries take practice, and practice happens over time. Integrating boundaries is a matter of compassionately understanding why they're so difficult, and establishing positive habits. One of the best ways to support yourself as you begin to set new boundaries is to consistently practice self-care, as you'll learn to do in this chapter.

Getting Comfortable with Uncomfortable Emotions

Boundary-keeping, like any habit, is a trade-off between immediate benefit and long-term reward. Over the long haul, the well-defined life will pay off in any number of ways, with better health, better relationships, better balance in how you spend your time, and other ways. But those long-term rewards are hard to remember in the pressure of the moment. In the short term, we're often rewarded for abandoning our boundaries. If we give in to temptation, we're rewarded with indulgence. If we give in to the pressure of someone else's expectations, we're rewarded for pleasing them, which soothes us.

Boundary-setting inevitably requires us to get more comfortable with uncomfortable emotions. These uncomfortable emotions include shame, embarrassment, guilt, remorse, sadness, and fear. If we've spent a lot of effort in our lives trying to avoid these emotions, it may seem counterintuitive to now seek greater understanding and acceptance of them. But some part of us may know that in the end we can't outrun these emotions. At some point, in a way and at a pace we can handle, we need to learn to tolerate them, if only so that they don't wreck our efforts to hold our boundaries, and thereby run our lives.

Shame and Embarrassment

Jimin and his boss were eating lunch when the boss said, "I hear you're a football fan." Jimin said, "Oh, yeah!" The boss grinned. "So," he said, "what did you think about how the Packers game ended last Sunday?" The truth was, Jimin didn't follow football. He had no idea how the Packers game had ended. He was flooded with embarrassment, then shame. Jimin took pride in his honesty, but now he'd been caught in a lie.

Social standing is linked to embarrassment. If Jimin had a conversation on the same topic with a neighborhood kid, it wouldn't have been the same as the one he had with his boss. If embarrassment comes from imperiled social standing, shame makes us doubt our own worth. Embarrassment happens only in public; shame can arise in private.

Shame thrives in silence, so a healthy response to shame is to talk about it. We can talk about it best in a setting that we know to be safe. Because shame tells a false either/or story (either you're honorable and admirable or you're utterly worthless), it can be useful to explore gray areas, if only to weaken shame's grip. And it really helps decouple what you've done from who you are. Maybe you have done something you're disappointed by, but that's different from who you are.

Guilt and Remorse

If shame says, "I feel bad because I am bad," guilt says, "I feel bad because I've done something bad." Shame is unhealthy and unproductive, but guilt can be incredibly productive. We are moral creatures. We know the difference between right and wrong. We know our actions affect other people, even unintentionally.

Janai's friend Ginger told her excitedly that their favorite band was coming to town. Janai went online and bought a ticket. Unfortunately, it was the last one. Now Ginger couldn't go. Ginger asked to buy the ticket from her. But Janai, working on her boundaries, said, "No, I'm sorry."

That weekend at the show, Janai felt guilty. On the one hand, she was trying to be less of a pushover. Ginger's failure to buy a ticket in time wasn't her responsibility. On the other hand, Ginger would've loved the show, and friends help each other out.

Guilt is rarely an open-and-shut case. We need to think through competing values and decide: Is our discomfort because someone else is disappointed in us, or because we are? It's a helpful dilemma. If guilt is the recognition that we've done something wrong, remorse is the next step. It leads us to apologize and seek repair.

Sadness

Omar's drinking buddies were all going out to a bar. But Omar was going to be sitting at home. The week before, he'd realized he needed to stop drinking. It was excruciating telling his friends. One got angry, accusing him of judging them. Another pleaded with him to go out just one more time. But Omar held firm. Drinking wasn't safe for him anymore.

Now he was home alone. He was proud of his decision. But he was incredibly sad. His new boundary would mean spending less time with these people and maybe even losing them as friends. It was uncomfortable feeling that sadness. But he knew that in the past he'd handled uncomfortable feelings by drinking. Now he knew he needed to listen to what the sadness was telling him about what was important and what was changing in himself.

Finding a way to talk about sadness and to think about it helps put it in perspective. Omar called up his sister to tell her how he was feeling. The rewards of a boundary will almost always come with some loss from our previous boundaryless life. It's okay to feel sad. Thinking about it, naming it, and finding someone to share it with helps.

Fear

Deborah was two months out of her marriage. Even though it had been her decision to get a divorce, she felt fear almost constantly. What was happening? Hadn't she wanted this? Still, there were so many things she'd relied on from her ex. Now she was out in the world on her own.

Boundarylessness is a survival strategy that says, "If I put others first, I won't be in danger. My safety relies on them being okay." So it makes sense that when we set firm boundaries—no longer relying on others as much for safety—we might also feel fear. Fear alerts us to a threat, so we can respond in ways that promote our survival. However, that helpful evolutionary mechanism now often takes the form of chronic anxiety.

When we've set a boundary, or are considering setting one, we can expect fear. But fear is a signal, not a fact. It's merely saying, "Hey! Check this out." If we can self-regulate, through breathing exercises, meditation, or something else, and dial down our anxiety, we can thoughtfully respond to that signal. Maybe it's helpfully orienting us to a challenge. But often it will be only a habitual reaction, playing out an old script.

BOUNDARIES IN PRACTICE

Nazira had just come back from visiting the apartment next door, where she'd politely told her new neighbors to turn down their music. It was after midnight! She knew she was right, not just morally but also according to the lease that everyone signed. But she couldn't stop shaking. What if they retaliated? Or started up the music again? Would she look like a fool? She made some tea, sat at the kitchen table, and began to write in her journal. Self-soothing and finding words to describe your experience and confirm your commitments can help when setting boundaries floods you with strong feelings.

THE FEELING WHEEL

So often, strong feelings can overtake us, flooding our capacity to think clearly. In 1982, Gloria Willcox created the Feeling Wheel to help people identify and name the emotion they were experiencing. As you look at the Feeling Wheel, see if you can find a name for what you're feeling. You might start toward the center with a more general category of emotion, and then move outward to get more specific. When you have specific language for what you are feeling, you can make a more thoughtful and specific choice about how to respond.

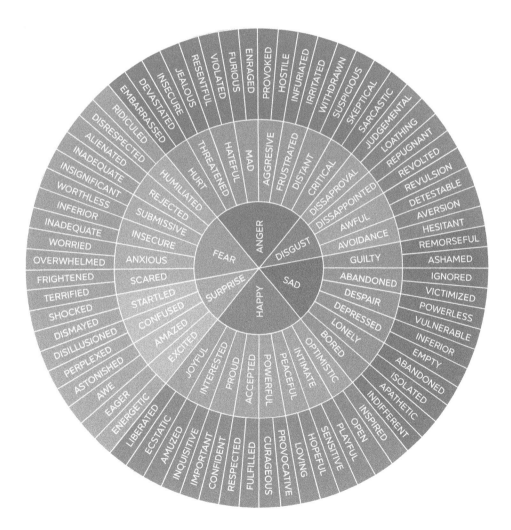

THE DEAR MAN SKILL

Dialectical behavior therapy teaches clients practical skills for engaging life's challenges. One skill for managing and communicating about strong emotions is known by the acronym DEAR MAN. When you experience a strong feeling related to a boundary or a boundary violation, DEAR MAN describes steps you can take to engage someone else with clarity and courage in a difficult and/or emotional situation or relationship:

◆ **D**escribe: In terms as factual and objective as possible, describe the situation—the events and their context—simply and clearly. This answers the question "what."

◆ **E**xpress: Using "I" language, express how you feel.

◆ **A**ssert: Advocate for your needs. Again, in "I" statements, you can say, "I need_____."

◆ **R**einforce: If you're receiving support, acknowledge it. Reinforce what's working.

◆ **M**indful: Anxiety may distract you. Don't let it. Even if you need to rely on a script or talking points as you speak, stay emotionally present.

◆ **A**ppear: Note your body language. Keep it confident, with direct eye contact.

◆ **N**egotiate: When you've expressed your feelings and needs, it may be difficult, but also helpful, to hear and receive the other person's experience—their feelings and needs—so you perhaps can work collaboratively toward a new solution. Assess whether this is the right time for that or whether you'll agree to work on it later. (This assumes you are working within a functional relationship. If it's an abusive one, don't engage in negotiation.)

For this exercise, think of a particular situation that stirs strong feelings in you. In the spaces, follow the DEAR MAN sequence to see how you could apply it. For now, you are only writing out a scenario you can imagine and would predict in this brave and challenging encounter. After the thought exercise, assess: Is this an actual encounter you would like to enact? If so, give it a try!

◆ **D**escribe:

....

....

....

◆ **E**xpress:

....

....

....

◆ **A**ssert:

....

....

....

◆ **R**einforce:

....

....

....

◆ **M**indful:

....

....

....

- ◆ **A**ppear:

....

....

....

- ◆ **N**egotiate:

....

....

....

Prioritize You

Jack worked hard to provide for his family. But the years of overwork had come at a cost. He'd neglected his body, he'd abandoned his personal goals, and he saw in the mirror the eyes of someone who'd sacrificed too much. Things had to change.

First, he negotiated with his boss at work, asking for clearer responsibilities. To his surprise, his boss readily agreed. Then he asked his wife to support him in making some changes with his diet, health, and exercise. She said, "Of course!" But nothing changed. He was still overfunctioning. He realized he couldn't ask others to be responsible for making him change; it was up to him.

Jack had always been reflective, and now he realized that he was still internalizing his father's wisecracks about being lazy. It took some time, but he found a way to let his father know that he wouldn't be laughing off those hurtful comments anymore. At work, he let people know that he would no longer cover their mistakes. Some reacted poorly, but he had expected that, and he regulated his anxiety in the face of their disappointment and anger. He realized that was the cost of advocating for himself. He began saying "no" to the incessant demand for volunteer roles at church. He liked to sing in the choir, and that's what he would do. Saying "no" was so hard for him. He was used to being able to squeeze everything in.

If he was going to make changes in his diet and health, he knew he had to create and sustain new habits; it couldn't just be wishful thinking or sheer willpower. So he made a plan for self-care with a lot of repetition, to develop automaticity, which is when habits become so ingrained that they are automatic. Going on hikes gave him both exercise and the solitude he had craved. It was time and space for himself—no one else.

He learned to be patient with himself, to forgive his lapses, and to continue to steer toward the life that he wanted, one in which he finally put himself first. To his surprise, the radiance and health that this "selfishness" produced seemed to delight others, as well.

TRACK YOUR HABITS FOR A WEEK

When working on bringing about a change in your life, developing external support can be helpful: things like accountability partners and little prizes at the end of successful periods. One support mechanism that can help your progress is a habit tracker. It's just a simple form where you record whether you did what you intended to do in a particular realm on a particular day.

Choose only five or six habits to track at first, or perhaps only two or three. You're building your habit muscle, not trying to fix everything at once. If the accountability of seeing the box to check heightens your focus and provides a little incentive, that's great. You can even celebrate at the end of the week for checking all (or most) of your boxes. However, if a habit tracker begins to be more important than the habit itself, try something else. Keep it light! You're learning. Here's an example of a habit tracker.

	DAY 1	DAY 2	DAY 3	DAY 4	DAY 5	DAY 6	DAY 7
Example: Drank 8 glasses of water a day	✓	✓		✓	✓	✓	

USING POSITIVE PSYCHOLOGY

Positive psychology encourages a focus on vision, goals, and strengths to help us orient ourselves toward what we want rather than persist in focusing on problems, which can, perversely, reinforce them. That's the framework of this exercise: to reinforce your intentions by inviting you to find language for the strength and resources you'll bring to this effort. Use these prompts to help practice positive psychology in your own life:

1. Describe a time when something was hard, but you found a way to do what you wanted to do.

....

....

....

2. Think of a challenge you met successfully. What strengths within yourself did you use to achieve that success?

_____

_____

_____

3. What are three gifts of yours (for example, *sense of humor*, *work ethic*, and *emotional intelligence*)? How will those gifts be useful in your effort to put yourself first?

_____

_____

_____

4. What's something you take for granted now in your life, but that seemed daunting—if not impossible—earlier in your life? Do some hard thinking: How did you do it?

_____

_____

_____

5. Because celebration helps reinforce learning retention, as you move through this period of discovery and growth, how will you celebrate at different milestones?

_____

_____

_____

Key Takeaways

If boundary-setting and boundary-keeping were easy, we wouldn't need to think so much about them and to make hard, brave choices about them. But, as we discussed in this chapter, engaging our deepest needs and fears can be a challenge. Review these key ideas from this chapter to reinforce your learning.

1. Setting boundaries delivers long-term rewards, but abandoning our boundaries in the heat of the moment gives immediate relief. It's important to be clear about which we're choosing.

2. Embarrassment is when our social standing is at risk; shame is when our sense of worth is at risk. Calming ourselves down to think about each more reasonably will help us better see what's happening.

3. Although it doesn't feel good, guilt can be a helpful emotion, asking us to consider our part in a moral problem. If we see we've done wrong and want to make things right, a good first step is to express remorse.

4. Sadness and fear are natural emotions that arise when we let go of the life we had for the one we now choose.

5. Putting ourselves first isn't something someone can do for us; we have to do it ourselves. It takes patient diligence, but it's possible—and infinitely rewarding.

CHAPTER 7

Maintaining Your Boundaries

To remain stable, you must change. It's one of life's paradoxes. To maintain your boundaries, you must stay alert to changes in the environment, in relationships, and in yourself. Sometimes, upholding the same values in the face of dramatic change around or within yourself means adapting to or updating your boundaries. What was true and important for you in young adulthood may no longer be true in middle age. So boundaries aren't a process of "set it and forget it." They are mindfully developed, mindfully sustained, and sometimes mindfully changed over time.

Your Digital Relationships

A high school history teacher was at home at night with her kids when her phone buzzed. It was a text: "What's the reading assignment for tonight?" What seemed to her like a violation of her privacy at home seemed normal to one of her students. Years ago, boundaries of time and space were more clearly defined: If you were at home, you were unreachable. Now technology has opened up round-the-clock access to one another and there are different perspectives about what's appropriate or not. Rather than relying on current norms, it's up to us to intentionally decide and communicate when we're available and when we are not.

Technology

People put their phones down when they go to sleep. When they wake up, the first thing they reach for is their phones. Technology pervades our lives. There are benefits: For example, a watch that monitors our heart rate can alert us to trouble. But the urgency created by a digital landscape, and communication strategies designed to hook our attention, can make it difficult for us to maintain healthy boundaries.

Technology benefits our lives, but without boundaries, it can be corrosive. Boundaries make sure we use technology and it doesn't use us.

It's important to reflect on your relationship with technology. How much of your engagement with it is mindful and deliberately chosen? How much is automatic and compulsive? A good test is to go for a day without engaging with technology the way you usually do, and observe your anxiety level. If your anxiety rises with even the thought of such an experiment, then setting some mindful boundaries might be helpful.

For example, emails and texts are efficient ways to be in touch with others, but they can be engines of distraction. So can you set boundaries on when you'll check emails and texts and when you won't? Are there hours at night after which you can't be reached? What boundaries can you set about response time? Online news can be compelling, but can you limit your intake of news to certain times of the day, instead of scrolling and scrolling? What boundaries would you set on that front?

WHERE DO YOU STAND WITH TECHNOLOGY?

Because technology is so deeply embedded in our lives, take this quiz to raise your awareness about your relationship with technology, so that you're in a position to make some choices about it. The quiz is in the format of True/False statements. As with all the exercises in this book, there's no grade or "getting it wrong." This is merely self-assessment, so that you're more aware.

1.	Every day I spend at least two hours away from my phone.	True	False
2.	In the past month I've gone two days in a row without answering email.	True	False
3.	Knowing that online news is designed to hook me, I have intentional ways of engaging it, and of stopping that engagement without mindlessly scrolling.	True	False
4.	When I'm anxious, one way I soothe myself is by engaging with online content.	True	False
5.	I stick to my decisions about who may track my online activity and how.	True	False
6.	I'm sensitive to the urgency of others regarding my response time.	True	False
7.	My boundaries for texting are clear and consistent regarding who, how, when, and how much.	True	False
8.	My online activity and engagement with technology doesn't interfere with my important life goals.	True	False
9.	At least half my waking hours are spent engaged with technology.	True	False

Based on your self-assessment, you may have new awareness of your current relationship with technology. Take a moment to write down some initial intentions, which you may choose to develop into boundaries.

1. With regard to social media, three things I will do are:

....

....

....

2. With regard to social media, three things I won't do are:

....

....

....

3. When it comes to engaging technology, one thing I will be sure to do is:

....

4. When it comes to engaging technology, one thing I will be sure not to do is:

....

Responding to Boundary Violations

Karina worked best with an orderly work space. Because she always made sure to inventory her supplies, she never ran out of what she needed. Her coworker, Mika, though, seemed to think Karina's desk was a stationery store. He'd nab a pen or a sticky note as he walked by. It wasn't the financial cost that upset Karina, it was Mika's presumption. She had told him her boundaries, but he'd claim he forgot or that he "really needed it." Because boundaries express our selfhood and dignity, even seemingly trivial boundary violations are wounding, tapping into deeper anxieties about our autonomy and our safety.

Standing Firm

If boundary violations were simple, committed by villains, they'd be easier to recognize and address. But more often we experience boundary violations from those we like and trust—those we've chosen to spend our time with. Often, transgressors don't intend to harm us. It's just that they have their own needs, fears, and drives, and in their internal calculations, those override their awareness of, and concern for, our boundaries.

Ironically, the person protecting their own boundaries may be the one who's socially punished. Others may call them "uptight," "selfish," or even "cruel" for not allowing the transgression to pass without comment. This reaction is less about the transgression than it is an expression of the need to keep the peace and maintain the fiction that all's well regardless of what happens. The one holding to their boundary may actually have a similar response, wondering if they're being too harsh.

It's important to anticipate and recognize these dynamics that can undermine boundary-keeping. This helps you prepare to stand firm. One set of strategies is cultivating support for your boundaries. These would include practices such as journaling or visualization that reinforce the importance of your boundaries, as well as developing accountability partners with whom you can check in. It's even helpful to form a community of others who share this boundary (people in addiction recovery know all about this).

Another set of strategies are related to incidents of transgression. If possible, name the transgression in the moment (it helps to think of how you'll do that; what words you might use). However, even if you're unable to name it in the moment, you have the right to address the transgression after the fact, to seek dialogue or simply the chance to reassert the boundary.

A CHECKLIST FOR MAINTAINING BOUNDARIES

Standing firm can be confusing and you can begin to doubt yourself. For this exercise, think of one particular boundary you'd like to explore. Use this checklist to assess your current situation and get some objective clarity about where you and others stand in relation to that boundary.

☐ I am clear and confident that my boundary is right for me.
☐ My boundary agrees with my values and my identity.
☐ I have articulated this boundary to others.

- ☐ I have behaved in ways that express this boundary.
- ☐ I have articulated consequences to others for not respecting this boundary.
- ☐ The consequences fall primarily on violators, not on me.
- ☐ People sometimes question this boundary, not from curiosity but in an effort to change it.
- ☐ People to whom I've expressed the boundary, verbally and with my behavior, still violate this boundary.
- ☐ Bystanders actively support the violation.
- ☐ Bystanders may not support the violation, but they're more interested in keeping the peace.
- ☐ I have support for challenging the violation.
- ☐ I have a plan for addressing the violation.
- ☐ The behavior of others has made me doubt myself. But on further reflection, I'm clear in my boundary.

After completing this inventory of your relationship to boundaries, consequences, violators, and bystanders, you may have a more objective and accurate view of a complex situation involving your boundaries. Hopefully, you've identified areas of strength, where things are as you'd like them to be. But you may have also identified areas that need your attention and creative, courageous response. Take the time you need, but be sure to address them.

HELPFUL PHRASES

It can be such a challenge to confront someone else about their violation of your boundaries, especially when it's someone you generally like, in a relationship you're generally happy about, and the boundary—at least to others—may seem to be of little consequence. And yet, because it's your boundary, and because its violation is damaging to your integrity, you're willing to address the wrong and advocate for your boundaries to be respected. But how? Here's a list of phrases that can help in a conversation in which you reassert your boundaries:

- ◆ I'd like to have a conversation about something that matters to me.
- ◆ I'm not comfortable with_____.
- ◆ I'm not willing to_____.
- ◆ What I'm asking you is_____.
- ◆ Here's what I need_____.

- ◆ Here's what I'm going to do_____.
- ◆ This doesn't work for me.
- ◆ I've decided that_____.
- ◆ I'm not going to justify or defend it. It's my choice that_____.
- ◆ If it happens again, what I've decided is_____.
- ◆ I value our relationship, and I also value my dignity, so_____.
- ◆ I've decided to take part in relationships where I'm respected, and_____.
- ◆ This is hard for me to say, but it's also important, so_____.
- ◆ I've been avoiding this conversation for a while, but I can't anymore.

Removing Toxicity

Most boundary violations from others are unwitting and can be resolved with a simple, direct conversation. But some boundary violations are recurrent, despite your repeated attempts to clearly state the boundary so the violator understands.

From the start, it can be helpful to reframe the exercise of responding to such disrespect as something that's in your own interests. For example, rather than thinking, "I wish I didn't have to have a difficult conversation," you could think, "I want to be strong in my boundaries. A difficult conversation is an opportunity to learn and get stronger, which will help me in other areas of my life." (Boundary-setting is a selfish practice in the healthiest sense of the term.) To be clear, we're talking about a situation in which your boundaries have been clearly expressed already and have been ignored. Don't focus too much on the violator's motivation; focus on their behavior.

Before engaging with them, ask yourself, "Given that this person hasn't respected important boundaries, am I safe confronting them or could their response be harmful to me?" You need not be a martyr; choosing a safe setting and means of engaging the violator will help. In this light, ask yourself, "Do I want to engage this person alone, or will I recruit someone else to be involved?" A third party could be someone you both know or a friend of yours. But it could also be a mediator, a clergyperson, a therapist, or a lawyer.

Next, ask yourself, "Although I have articulated the boundary clearly, have I also articulated the consequence of violating the boundary and enacted that consequence?" As discussed earlier, the consequence should fall heaviest on the violator, not the violated. And the mere threat of it is ineffective; it's the enactment that works.

If the consequence has been enacted but the transgression hasn't stopped, ask yourself, "What consequence would shift the violator's calculation about committing the transgression? Is there a way to turn up the heat?"

If you have clearly reasserted your boundaries and the consequences for violation, have "turned up the heat" of the consequences, and have even brought in a third party, all to no avail, upholding your boundaries can mean choosing to cease contact with that person for a defined period, for an open-ended period, or until certain conditions are met. Often, this cutoff will be the first choice someone makes, but if it's chosen too quickly without the steps mentioned here, you may find yourself unsettled and vigilant, rather than at peace.

WELLNESS RECOVERY ACTION PLAN

Mental health educator and author Mary Ellen Copeland developed the Wellness Recovery Action Plan (WRAP) for people in the midst of struggle—for instance, a relationship in which boundaries have been disrespected. WRAP has several dimensions: developing a daily maintenance plan, understanding triggers and what to do in response to them, identifying early warning signs that things are breaking down and having an action plan, and crisis planning. You can find more about it online. For this exercise, however, we'll focus on the first dimension: developing a daily maintenance plan. Write down your thoughts about these statements:

1. Some habits and relationships that support my wellness are:

2. The things that are meaningful to me, inspire me, and remind me of my values are:

3. Some things that I will test to see if they support my wellness are:

4. Setting my baseline—when I'm well, what am I like? How can I tell?

5. What do I need to do for myself daily to keep feeling as well as possible?

6. What do I need to do less often than daily to sustain my wellness?

7. What I know I need to do to sustain my well-being, but often don't do for some reason, is:

STRENGTHENING CONSEQUENCES

In a scenario where someone has repeatedly disrespected your boundaries, it can be helpful to clarify or even sharpen the consequences, making sure that the consequences fall heaviest on the violator, not on you. For those who've spent much of their lives protecting other people, imagining consequences, let alone implementing them, can be a challenge.

This exercise has a few steps.

First, identify an important boundary of yours that has been violated.

Say whom it was violated by and how.

Now, in the following table, brainstorm 10 consequences if this boundary is violated again. After you've gotten all 10, rank them in the order in which you might implement them. Some will be absurd, in the spirit of brainstorming. But choose at least five that you can imagine actually implementing.

POSSIBLE CONSEQUENCES	RANK

POSSIBLE CONSEQUENCES	RANK

Reassessing Your Boundaries

When her kids were teenagers, Jo loved that they and their friends would hang out in the basement, gobbling up the snacks she provided, playing video games, and being goofy. When they were in college, they kept coming over, and it was nice to stay in touch. But now the gang was in their late twenties. Most had professional jobs. Some were even married. What had been joyful visits before now were irritating.

Still, Jo was conflicted. Would setting a new boundary chase them away? She wanted to keep in touch. And was she sending a mixed message? For years she'd told her kids and all their friends that her house was a safe place for them and that they were always welcome. But cleaning up corn chips and beer cans left behind by young professionals wasn't part of the deal.

Because articulating and practicing boundaries can require so much of us—because boundaries are so hard won—we can be loath to question or change them. But if we don't remain alert and aware, and adjust them as needed, once-reasonable boundaries can become rigid or porous from our neglect. If old boundaries begin to nag at you, that's perfectly normal. It's an invitation to reflect.

These could be boundaries in your personal life that you maintain yourself, such as with your diet, exercise, or sleep. Or they could be boundaries that are upheld in the context of relationships—for instance, what you are and are not willing to do, and the behavior you're willing or not willing to tolerate from others. If the boundaries were settled and satisfactory before, ask yourself what has changed: the conditions, the relationship, your tolerance, your values, you? See what's different now.

Next, without dismissing the boundaries that were appropriate in the past in that context, think about what boundaries work for you now, as things are. What are you willing to do or tolerate, and what are you not? Out of frustration, you may be tempted to take an either/or stance. More likely, what's appropriate is some mindful middle ground.

When you're clear about what you want now, if the boundary is in the context of a relationship, it's time to raise the matter with others. Again, it's perfectly normal to renegotiate. You can even start with one of my favorite expressions for renegotiating boundaries: "You know, I've been thinking _____."

HOW HAVE YOUR BOUNDARIES CHANGED?

You may already have updated old boundaries without realizing it. To gain awareness of how much you have altered your boundaries, this exercise asks you to consider your boundaries from 10 years ago and compare them to your boundaries now. The last column is for any reflections you might have on when, how, and why you adjusted that boundary. If you notice a theme in that reflection column, it could be a useful insight into your own process for updating boundaries.

TYPE OF BOUNDARY	10 YEARS AGO	NOW	REFLECTION
Physical (health, diet, exercise, etc.)			
Intellectual			
Emotional			
Material			
Sexual			

Continued ➤

Continued ➤

TYPE OF BOUNDARY	10 YEARS AGO	NOW	REFLECTION
Financial			
Time			

HONORING YOUR LIFE VISION

Use these writing prompts to gain clarity on a boundary that you're reassessing and may update soon:

1. The longtime boundary I've lived with is:

_____

_____

2. The reason that boundary made sense in the past was:

_____

_____

_____

3. Even though I've valued life with that boundary, more recently my observation has been:

_____

_____

4. My vision for my life these days is:

_____

_____

5. I'm not willing to live by that earlier boundary any longer because:

_____

_____

6. As I think about it, a reasonable new boundary for this situation is:

_____

_____

7. The new boundary serves my current situation and vision for my life because:

_____

_____

8. I will articulate this new boundary with others in the following manner:

_____

_____

EMBRACING POSSIBILITY

Lisa Lahey and Robert Kegan, codevelopers of the Immunity to Change framework (a way to work through unconscious assumptions), suggest that any resistance we might have to desired change isn't pathological, but rather, it is logical. The resistance is protecting something that feels threatened by the potential change. The fear in the resistance says, "It's one or the other: this change or else the thing I'm protecting." Lahey and Kegan developed the Immunity to Change process in response, to help a person think through and honor their own resistance while showing that a both/and future is possible. You can find resources related to Immunity to Change in bookstores and online. But a simplified version is to respond to the following questions:

1. What is my desired change, to which I've committed? (For example, *I won't binge on snacks late at night.*)

2. What is my actual behavior regarding my desired change? (For example, *This week, I binged on snacks after 9 p.m. on Monday, Wednesday, and Thursday.*)

3. For each behavior in question 2, what is the hidden competing commitment? (For example, *I have the right to soothe myself after a stressful day, and bingeing on snacks is a way to self-soothe.*)

_____

_____

_____

_____

4. What assumptions underlie what I've written in question 3? (For example, *If I don't binge on snacks at night, I won't be soothed and would be disrespecting my right to self-soothe.*)

_____

_____

_____

_____

When you've written everything out—both your explicit intentions and your inner resistance, along with some thoughts about what might be driving that resistance—you can investigate your assumptions and move toward a both/and future that serves your integrity and no longer hamstrings you with an either/or dilemma. For instance, in the example I used in the exercise here, a person might explore how they can honor their commitment not to binge on snacks late at night and also assert their right to self-soothe, rather than choosing between one or the other.

Key Takeaways

As you think about this final chapter, keep in mind these key ideas:

1. Technology is pervasive. If we don't set some boundaries on how we use it, we can be sure that it is using us. Make choices about how you will and won't engage with the tech in your life.

2. Social media can connect us but it can also heighten insecurity. Firm boundaries about social media promote mental health.

3. In response to a boundary violation, check your consequences. Have you implemented them in a way in which they fall on the violator?

4. As you reassert boundaries that have been disrespected, consider whether the presence of a third party will help.

5. Persistent boundary violations are inexcusable. You have the right to increase the consequences and then, ultimately, to sever contact.

6. It's normal and important to reassess boundaries through life, as things change. Ask yourself what has changed: conditions, the relationship, your tolerance, your values, you? Any of these is a legitimate reason to update your boundaries.

A FINAL WORD

Congratulations on completing this workbook! Many people decide that charting the course for their own lives is too hard, and that they'd rather continue pleasing or soothing others, even when they feel resentful inside. But not you! For reasons important to you, you have decided to do the hard, necessary work of defining your life more clearly, understanding your purpose and your goals, and setting the boundaries that will be required to maintain your focus on what your life is about.

Different people are ready to do this hard thing at different points in their lives. Some will have traveled through some fairly low times before they're ready for better boundaries. Don't mourn the past or dwell on disappointments for too long. Instead, celebrate what you've accomplished now and will continue to work on. Remember, celebration helps reinforce learning and strengthens what you've gained.

Articulating and setting boundaries is only the first step. Maintaining them, especially in the face of challenging dynamics and relationships, will take mindful, ongoing engagement. You'll discover, in time, that revisiting long-established boundaries helps keep your intention and connection with them fresh. Sometimes that will mean updating old boundaries so that they serve your life now.

A well-defined life with clear boundaries dramatically changes a person. You'll feel stronger, more energized, better able to think for yourself. But you may notice that conditions and relationships that served a less-boundaried life no longer serve you. People often find that relationships with others who also uphold clear boundaries—whether or not they're the same boundaries as yours—are more attractive now than relationships with others who don't. It's normal and natural that a changed life will have a ripple effect on the choices you make and the friends and circumstances you choose.

I wish you the best of luck going forward. No longer are you fated to an anxious, fearful life driven by the demands of others. Now you claim the adventure of growth and vitality. Enjoy the discipline of keeping clear, mindful, and true to your commitments, knowing that they'll change as you continue to change.

RESOURCES

Books

The Assertiveness Guide for Women, Julie de Azevedo Hanks
Strategies for women based on mindfulness and cognitive behavioral therapy.

The Body Keeps the Score, Bessel van der Kolk
Examining the impact of trauma on the brain and mental health.

Boundaries at Work, Henry Cloud
More on setting and enforcing workplace boundaries.

Boundary Boss, Terri Cole
How to respond to your boundary blueprint with self-awareness, acceptance, and compassion.

Codependent No More: How to Stop Controlling Others and Start Caring for Yourself, Melody Beattie
A book that addresses some deeper issues related to boundary-setting.

Don't Touch My Hair!, Sharee Miller
A picture book for kids on setting boundaries early in life.

The Eight Concepts of Bowen Theory, Roberta Gilbert
An introduction to a theory promoting the capacity to live clearer, more coherent lives.

It Didn't Start with You, Mark Wolynn
A book on the impact of inherited family trauma and boundary-setting with family members.

Practicing Mindfulness, Matthew Sockolov
A book with 75 exercises that promote greater mindfulness and self-regulation.

Toxic Parents: Overcoming Their Hurtful Legacy and Reclaiming Your Life, Susan Forward
A guide for adult children of difficult parents.

***Where to Draw the Line: How to Set Healthy Boundaries Every Day*,**
Anne Katherine
Case studies and methods for setting healthy boundaries in many areas of our lives.

Finding a Therapist

The Bowen Center for the Study of the Family
TheBowenCenter.org

The hub of a network of training centers and clinics that promote Bowen Family Systems Theory, a model that helps people live more clearly defined and well-boundaried lives.

The Center for Trauma & Resilience
TraumaHealth.org

A nonprofit organization offering a range of programs and services for those who have experienced trauma.

Psychology Today
PsychologyToday.com

Psychology Today maintains a directory of local therapists that you can search for particular credentials or specializations. Often, people try working with two or three therapists before settling into a long-term therapeutic relationship.

INDEX

ACKNOWLEDGMENTS

Writing a book can challenge not only an author's personal boundaries, but also those of the people around them. So, it's with humility and gratitude that I thank my wife, Molly, and our kids for their generosity and grace through the writing process, and for holding me accountable to the person I'm trying to be. In a similar light, I'm also grateful for a patient and compassionate editor, Adrian Potts. And for the skilled work of administrative assistant Jordyn Joy. Thanks, as well, to friends and loved ones who have shown me what it means to live a life of honesty and integrity, upheld by clear boundaries.

ABOUT THE AUTHOR

 **Jake Morrill,** LMFT, is a therapist and leadership coach, supporting people to be brave, clear, and effective in relationships at work and at home. He holds degrees from Harvard Divinity School and the Iowa Writers' Workshop. An associate faculty member at the Bowen Center for the Study of the Family and a frequent presenter on Bowen Family Systems Theory, he's the author of four previous books. To learn more or to explore a coaching or consulting relationship with Jake, go to JakeMorrill.com.